SUPER PARTY GAMES

Fun &
Original
Ideas
for 10 or
More

John Chaneski

Illustrated by Kimble Pendleton Mead

Sterling Publishing Co., Inc.
New York

793.2
CHA

*To my favorite big, fun group: Mom, Dad, Gram, Nannie,
Bobby, Alison, Chris, Mary Ann, Christian, and Alyssa.*

Library of Congress Cataloging-in-Publication Data Available

2 4 6 8 10 9 7 5 3 1

Published by Sterling Publishing Company, Inc.
387 Park Avenue South, New York, N.Y. 10016
© 1999 by John Chaneski
Distributed in Canada by Sterling Publishing
℅ Canadian Manda Group, One Atlantic Avenue, Suite 105
Toronto, Ontario, Canada M6K 3E7
Distributed in Great Britain and Europe by Cassell PLC
Wellington House, 125 Strand, London WC2R 0BB, England
Distributed in Australia by Capricorn Link (Australia) Pty Ltd.
P.O. Box 6651, Baulkham Hills, Business Centre, NSW 2153, Australia

Sterling ISBN 0-8069-5915-0 Trade

Contents

Acknowledgments

Thanks to my editor Peter Gordon for this opportunity.

Special thanks to the brilliant game inventors whose names (and noms) are found in this book. Even those who merely tinker deserve a round of applause.

Extra-special thanks are reserved for those who helped me gather the games and seek out information. The facts belong to them, the mistakes are all mine: Eric Berman, Philip M. Cohen, Dean Howard, Ed Pegg, Jr., Henry Picciotto, James G. Propp, and Will Shortz.

Extra-super-special thanks to Frank for not coming downstairs on November 30.

Extra-double-super-special thanks go out to Martin and Elisa Eiger for all their help and for waiting at the mall.

Introduction

A puzzle is a one-player game.

Strategy games, like chess, are usually two-player games. The strategic skill of one player is pitted against that of another, head-to-head.

Most party games are for at least four players and introduce the particular joys and frustrations of team play. The rule here is usually the more the merrier. But almost all of these games have an upper limit for players because things can easily get out of hand when there are more than 10, 12, or 14. If everyone isn't involved at all times, they stop having fun and the game starts to break down.

So what do you do if you need to entertain a large or very large group of people for an evening? Are most people in the group doomed to be mere spectators while a few others have all the fun? Not at all. There are many exciting and challenging games for 10, 20, 30, or even 100 players. These games, if executed with care, wit, and attention to detail, will thrill and delight your restless crowd.

In the pages that follow, you'll find many different types of games, allowing you to suit the play to the players. Family reunions, conventions, church socials, club meetings, fund-raisers—all provide great opportunities to present the challenges and social interaction that people love about games. But it's up to you to decide which game is right for a particular group at a particular time.

You might even come up with ideas for group games of your own. Creativity is one of the best aspects of games. Every game in this book was at one time created or adapted from another source by a game lover. Feel free to adapt them to fit your specific needs. Experiment and come up with your own games. Send us any old or new games you may have found or created. We'd like to hear about them, perhaps publish them, and, most of all, play them!

The National Puzzlers' League and Equinox
Many of the games in this book were culled from those played by members of a group called the National Puzzlers' League at their annual conventions.

The NPL, founded in 1883, is the oldest surviving organization of puzzle enthusiasts in the world. It consists of nearly 500 people, from all walks of life, whose vocation and/or avocation is puzzles of different kinds. Members create puzzles for each other to solve, which are printed in their monthly newsletter, *The Enigma*. For more information on the National Puzzlers' League, check out their Web site at www. puzzlers.org.

The NPL convention, held each year in a different city in mid-July, is a long weekend of puzzle solving, puzzle composing, socializing, and playing games. Besides the formal group games like the ones in this book, members gather each afternoon and late into the night to enjoy board games, charades, and all sorts of intelligent play.

For many NPL members, group gaming is so much fun that once a year is not enough. In recent years, local mini-conventions or game parties have arisen in California, Massachusetts, New York, and New Jersey, created and hosted by NPLers from those areas and attended by members and non-members alike from all over. One of the most notable game gatherings, and the source of many of the games in this book, are the Equinox parties that are run in the San Francisco area twice a year.

An NPL tradition is each member's adoption of a nom de plume upon joining. A "nom" can be just a nickname, but many others use clever wordplay. In this book, a game created by an NPL member includes his or her nom in parentheses after the byline.

Index of Categories

Each game in this book falls into one or more of these categories:

Trivia games require players to recall facts.

Bluffing games ask players to fool their opponents into believing them and to determine who is being dishonest.

Mixers are games designed to get people out of their seats and talking to one another. Whether played by people who have just met or already know each other, the object is not to get everyone to meet everybody else, but to break the invisible wall that exists between them.

Team games require arranging the group into teams of two or more players.

Individual games have each person playing as an individual against every other person.

Noncompetitive or cooperative games have no winners or losers and usually require the group to work together to complete some challenging task.

Some games that are primarily team games can be adapted to individual play and vice versa. After the name of each game you'll find the name of the person who created it or adapted it from another source. You'll also find the type of game, the suggested number of players, and the approximate playing time. The materials list is not to be taken as gospel. Use your best judgment when putting together your game; do what you can to make it convenient, exciting, and fun for your players.

Limer-wrecks

by John Chaneski (Chainsaw)

Category: mixer/creative/team
Players: 20–100+ and one emcee
Playing time: 30 minutes or longer
Materials: oaktag, markers

Limer-wrecks is a fine mixer for a very large group, the larger the better. It also works for grouping people into random teams of four, if you need to do so for another game or purpose. Multiples of four people per group are ideal, but you can fudge it.

PREPARATION: A little research is required. You'll need one limerick for every four players. Decide how clean they need to be. We suggest scouring children's humor books or weeding out the cleaner ones from a collection of limericks. Once you've decided which ones to use, write them down and number them for later reference.

On a 3" × 28" strip of oaktag write the first line of a limerick in letters large enough to be easily read from a medium distance. Write your reference number for that limerick unobtrusively on the back. On a second strip of the same dimensions write the second line, but omit the reference number. Do the same with the third and fourth lines. If possible, use a different color oaktag for each line.

Do the same for all the other limericks. If you use strips of different colors, make sure you use the same color for all the first lines, another color for all the second lines, and so on. Keep these sets of four lines grouped together but *do not mix them up*. You will do that later.

BEFORE THE GAME: Check how many people are playing. If possible, add stragglers or team up two people to play as one until you have a multiple of four players per group: 20, 24, 28, etc. Once you know the total number of players, divide it by four. That's how many limericks you'll need (100 people will require 25 limericks). Put aside the extra ones. Now shuffle the strips. Give every player one strip either facedown or folded so it can't be read. Tell everyone not to look at the strips until the signal is given. Once everyone has a strip, give them the following instructions.

INSTRUCTIONS: Each player has one of the first four lines of a limerick. When you (or the emcee if it isn't you) give the signal, everyone looks at his or her line and then tries to finds the other three people who have lines from the same limerick (this will be easier if you've used colored strips). When the correct groupings have been established, players show you their strips for confirmation and to receive the next instructions.

Limericks consist of five lines with the rhyme scheme AABBA. Here's an example:

A frisky young fellow named John
Awakened and saw he was gone.
He couldn't be found
Though he looked all around
And searched for him hither and yon.

Once a group has correctly assembled the first four lines, the four players must come up with a fifth line. It isn't necessary to find the "correct" last line, since the idea is for the other players to judge each completed limerick based on originality, wit, and how well it works as a limerick.

RUNNING THE GAME: As the players seek each other out, gauge how well they are doing. If the game seems to be taking too long, help them by pointing out that (for instance) all the first lines are yellow, all the second lines are blue, and so on. As each group shows you what it's put together, check it by using the limerick list you prepared earlier and the reference number on the first-line strip.

SCORING: We suggest you have six winners. The first three teams to get together are awarded the first three places in the "Search Division." When the limericks have been completed, ask a representative from each team to read their limerick to the assembled players. Gauge the success of each one by the laughter or applause it generates. You may need to have the top five or so read again to determine a winner. Award first, second, and third places in the "Write Division." Feel free to single out teams for particularly clever (or even amazingly bad) limericks.

KEEP IN MIND: It's important to choose limericks with rhymes that are unusual and different from one another. If two limericks have a similar rhyme, make sure the context makes it clear which line goes with which limerick. It's also important that the context clearly links the first two lines to the second two lines, since that will be the only clue to matching them.

When all the teams have been assembled, set an appropriate time limit for writing the fifth line.

Word Trade Center

by John Chaneski

Category: mixer/word
Players: 12–100+ and one emcee
Playing time: 30–60 minutes
Materials: A pool of cards, each having a letter and a point value. Half of the cards are red, the other half black. You'll need 7 cards times the number of players, plus a few extras, red dot stickers, black dot stickers, notebooks for scorekeepers, bell

This game is great for intelligent people who love words, but it can be played by almost any group by adjusting the difficulty level. For a somewhat simpler (and faster) game, use cards of only one color and eliminate the dots of the other color. This means no scoring bonus for words of one color, since they'll all the same color. For an even simpler game, eliminate the point values on the letter cards, thus avoiding the long process of calculating scores.

PREPARATION: Determine how many letter cards you need and have that many on hand. Existing games with letter cards include Royalty (U.S. Game Systems), AlphaBlitz (Wizards of the Coast), Anagrams (Endless Games), and Palabra (Kondrick, Inc.). You can even use the tiles from a Scrabble game. To get things moving faster, deal hands of seven cards in advance and put them in envelopes. Seal the envelopes so players can't look at their hands before the game.

Ask a number of people to act as scorekeepers, one for every 25 or so players. Each should have a notebook and a pen to record players' names, words, and scores, if possible.

BEFORE THE GAME: Hand out the cards and instruction sheets to the players.

INSTRUCTIONS: Each player gets a hand of seven cards, which he or she may not look at until the bell rings to signal the start of the trading day. Players now looks at their letters and try to create a word using all seven of them. Those who can't do so must walk around the room and trade letters with other players to get the needed letters to make a word.

Up to three letters may be traded in a single transaction. An offered trade may be declined and alternate trades suggested. Players should not let anyone see their hands. After five minutes of trading, each player may, one time only, turn in all his or her cards for seven new ones.

When a word is created, it's brought to the scorekeeper for tallying. The scorekeeper records the player's name, word, and whether or not it is all one color. Once a word is registered, the player returns to the group to make new words. No word may be registered more than once

by the same player. New words must differ from the player's previous word by at least one letter.

When a word is registered, the player gets a red dot sticker, which must be conspicuously worn. If it's a bonus word (all letters the same color), the player receives, and must wear conspicuously, a black dot. Each new word earns another dot.

Each properly registered unique word earns the player 1 point, plus the sum of the word's letter values. Words that are all black or all red earn double points.

The player who registers the most words is named Best Trader, and the player who earns the most points is Best Scorer. If the Best Scorer and the Best Trader are one and the same, that player is declared Super Scorer Trader.

The trading day lasts 30 minutes. When the bell rings, signaling the end of the trading day, all trading must stop, though players may continue to register words.

RUNNING THE GAME: Keep track of the time after the trading starts, and watch for problems or rules violations. Be prepared to help the scorekeepers as well as players who want new hands. When time is up, ring the bell and tell everyone to stop trading.

WINNERS: The Best Trader can be determined easily by the number of dots each trader is wearing. Calculating the Best Scorer could take a few hours, depending on the number of players and how well they did. Be sure to tell the players about this before the game. You can save time by estimating during the game which 10 or so players have the highest scores and calculating only those scores.

Number's Racket

by Ed Pegg, Jr. (Χειρων)

Category: Mixer/math
Players: 12–100+ and one emcee
Playing time: 30–60 minutes
Materials: nametags, cheat sheets, pads of paper, pens or pencils

Few large groups would consider mathematics a recreational activity, but this game is not difficult and can be made even easier. Each player is assigned a number. They then walk around the room and construct a mathematical equation, using the other players' numbers as the quantities and their own number as the solution. For example, if Mike is 3, Peter 2, Elaine 1, Trip 27, Joel 28, and Leslie 5, then Joel could construct: Mike × Peter + Trip ÷ Elaine – Leslie = Self ($3 \times 2 + 27 \div 1 - 5 = 28$).

PREPARATION: On each nametag write a number from 1 to 99. Make sure the number is readable, but leave enough space for the player's name. If you assign numbers ahead of time, record the names and numbers to facilitate scoring. If not, you'll have to record the players' numbers while they're playing. This might be a good idea anyway, since there's little for you to do while the game is running unless you decide to play. If you hand out the nametags ahead of time, tell the players to keep them facedown until instructed to turn them over. Or you can give out the nametags only when the game actually starts.

It's probably a good idea to photocopy a number of cheat sheets to explain the rules and remind players of the mathematical operations used and their order. At the very least, somewhere in the room there should be a poster or blackboard with illustrative examples that the players can refer to during the game.

INSTRUCTIONS: Players try to construct equations in the form: A times B plus C divided by D minus E equals MY NUMBER. Addition, subtraction, multiplication, and division must each be used exactly once and A, B, C, D, and E must include the names of the people who have those numbers. A, B, C, D, and E must be different numbers.

The game can be simplified by customizing the equation. For younger players, you can omit multiplication and division. Teachers can use the game to reinforce concepts currently being studied. Or you can extend the game by requiring the winner to "solve himself" two or three times.

RUNNING THE GAME: Hand out the cheat sheets and explain the game. Once everyone understands the rules, give players their nametags (or instruct them to turn up the facedown tags you gave them earlier) and have them write their names on them if that hasn't already been done. They may begin as soon as they're ready or when you give a signal.

If you're running a formal, very competitive game, tell the players to hand you (or a designated judge) their completed equations. These should be numbered as they're handed in. The numbers can be used to determine winners after the equations have been checked for correctness.

Game length will depend on how you run it. If you want it to be very competitive, set a very short time limit and stop the game when the time elapses. For a more relaxed game, don't stop the game until everyone has solved an equation. In this case, slower players could seek the help of quicker players who've already constructed their equations. Whether or not this is legal is up to you, but we like the cooperative aspect.

SCORING: Remember that this is intended primarily as a mixer game. So long as there is plenty of player interaction, consider it a success.

If you're running a relaxed game, players' equations can be checked later. If you're able to check them immediately, determine a winner from the correct equations that have been handed in on time and announce the winners.

In a formal game, accept no more equations once time has been called. Instead of checking the equations yourself, ask the players, in order, to stand and recite their equations as you write them on a blackboard. This way, the group will determine the equation's validity.

Word Chain

by John Chaneski

Category: mixer/word/cooperative
Players: 12–50+ and one emcee
Playing time: 15–30 minutes
Materials: oaktag, markers, tape

This quick game gets people up and moving and speaking to one another. Word Chain can also have a dramatic ending if the word chain works out perfectly.

PREPARATION: You should have some facility with words, because this game requires you to prepare a chain of words that form a compound word or two-word phrase with the words before and after it. For example, TIME, CARD, BOARD, WALK, MAN, POWER, BOOK, END, GAME.

Your word chain needs as many words as there are players. It can't hurt to start with a longer chain than necessary; you can always lop excess words off either end. Write each word on an oaktag card measuring about 5" × 7". The word should be large enough to be easily read from about three feet away. Keep these cards in word-chain order so you can easily lop off a word or two or three or nine.

BEFORE THE GAME: Hand out the cards, facedown, to each player. If you're using place settings, you can have a card preset at each setting. In either case, remind players not to look at their cards. Each table should have enough tape for players to tape the cards to each other.

INSTRUCTIONS: Each player tapes his or her card to the back of the player to the right, who must not be allowed to see the word on the card. Each of these words can form a compound word or two-word phrase with the word before it and the word after it. Give an example like the one above, avoiding any of the words in your group's actual chain. If your chain is open-ended and not circular (see Options, below), remind the players that two of them will be "anchors" who link to only one person each because their words are the first and last words of the chain.

At the signal, players try to form themselves into a word chain that works. Players may not ask each other what is on their own back or give that information to anyone else. But a player can say, for instance, "You should stand next to her" or ask, "Does it work if I stand between him and her?" Players who figure out what word is on their back by noting what the neighbors are wearing should hold that information until later.

If everyone cooperates, they should form a workable word chain. When they're done, read out the words and see if the chain works. If it does, ask the players to link up by standing next to each other or holding hands.

DURING THE GAME: There's not much to do. If someone seems completely confused, do what you can to help. Make sure no one cheats!

FINISH: Starting at one end of the chain, go from player to player asking them if they know the word on their back. If they do, have them say it aloud. If they are correct, say so, then determine if the word is in the correct position in the chain. To do this, say the word and the following word aloud and ask the group if it works as a compound word or phrase. If so, move on. If not, you have two options:

1. If your group is relatively small and you have time, ask the players to rearrange themselves.

2. If your group is relatively large or if you don't have time, ask if anyone is standing next to a word that would fit better in place of the wrong word. The players involved then switch places.

OPTIONS: Instead of having "anchor" players, you can tape the first and last words of the chain at either side of the room and ask the players to link up between them.

If you feel particularly adventurous, you can create a circular word chain in which the last word links with the first. For example: TENNIS, ELBOW, GREASE, MONKEY, BUSINESS, CARD, TABLE, TENNIS. Though this version is more fun, it's not as flexible should you need to fit the number of words to the number of players. Use it only if you think you can adjust the chain or the number of players.

One "scoring" possibility is to keep track of the number of mistakes the group makes. A+ = no mistakes; A = one mistake; B+ = two mistakes; etc.

KEEP IN MIND: A mistake might not be a mistake! If your players discover an alternate workable word chain from the words you've created, don't freak out! Congratulate them on a job well done!

Nametag Acrostics

by Sharon Pedersen

Category: mixer/noncompetitive
Players: 12–100+ and one emcee
Playing time: 15–30 minutes
Materials: 5" × 7" cards, markers, pens/pencils, yarn

This is a very simple, very low-stress mixer.

PREPARATION: Although you will need nametags, those little "Hello, My Name Is" stickers don't work for this game. Have a table set up where people can make their own nametags using the 5" × 7" cards and markers. You should have holes already punched in the cards so that they can be hung around the neck using the yarn. Have a sign set up or tell the players to write their names in large block letters across the top of the cards, leaving plenty of space below.

INSTRUCTIONS: The idea is to learn not only the names of the others in the group but also a little more about them. Everyone needs a pen or pencil.

At your signal, players begin wandering around the room. When two people meet, one of them asks the other whether he or she has a specific attribute. This attribute will be an adjective that begins with a letter in that person's name. For example, someone might ask me, "Are you jolly?" To which I might say, "Yeah, I'm jolly sometimes!" Since the answer is yes, the person who asked me the question writes the word "jolly" on my nametag, beginning with the first letter of the word. Like this:

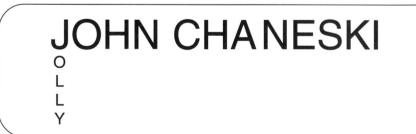

The object for each player is to obtain an adjective for each letter on his or her own nametag. The adjectives don't have to be gotten in order, but they all have to be obtained. Questions must be answered truthfully. If someone asks, "Are you punctual?" and you know you're not, you must admit it. Players may not write anything on their own nametags. Each player may get no more than one adjective from the same person; so everyone will have to circulate.

KEEP IN MIND: Some letters are troublesome, like X, Q, and Z. Since this is just a getting-to-know you game, there's no reason you shouldn't go around helping people fill out their nametag. Maybe two players together can try to figure out an appropriate adjective for a third player. Since "xenophilic" (loving strangers) and "xenophobic" (avoiding strangers) are just about the only two "x" adjectives available, allow your players to make that letter the second one in the word. This permits all sorts of adjectives, such as "exciting," "exacting," "exceptional," "expansive," or even the rather mundane "existing." While there may be a few "quiet" people around, many of them aren't game players. Try "quaint," "qualified," "quarrelsome," "quick," or "quirky." There may be a "zaftig" person in your group or a "zany," "zealous," or "zesty" type. At worst, there's a good chance that person might be "zippered" into whatever outfit he or she is wearing!

Your only other responsibility is to not let the game go on too long.

Peobble

by Jim Propp (Aesop)

Category: word/mixer/competitive
Players: 25–100+ and one emcee
Playing time: 30+ minutes
Materials: nametags, scoresheets, pens/pencils,
yellow dot stickers, red dot stickers

Peobble is Scrabble using people as tiles. Players represent letters. The object is to find the highest-scoring arrangement of people (letters). Collecting names as well as letters makes the game more personal.

PREPARATION: When the players enter, ask them to choose a letter from their name. This will be the letter they represent. That letter will be shown as a Scrabble tile, with the proper point value on it, either drawn or stuck to the nametag (in its proper position in the player's name).

This can be done in a few ways. As players enter and choose a letter, you can either ask someone to draw the name and tile on a nametag sticker or ask the players to draw it themselves. Be sure to have the correct point values for each letter at hand. Alternatively, you can print the nametags in advance, as well as the Scrabble tile stickers to add to the names. Simply write out or use your computer to print out letters and their point values onto sheets of adhesive labels and then cut them into the shape of Scrabble tiles. Make sure you have enough so that you won't run out of needed letters.

Have fun with the nametags! Here's how mine might look:

JOHN CH A₁ NESKI

About 20% of your players will also get a yellow dot on their nametag, indicating a Double Word Score space, and about 10% a red dot, indicating a Triple Word Score space. How you deal out the dots is up to you. You can dot people after they all have their tags or as they come in, or you can dot every fifth and tenth person. Dotting new-comers and guests insures that they will interact with other players.

You'll also need a scoring sheet for each person to remind them of the rules and provide a place to list words. Don't explain the reason for the tiles on the nametags until the game is about to start.

INSTRUCTIONS: Each player has a letter tile with a point value on his or her nametag. On your signal, players walk around trying to make the highest-scoring words using the letters on other players' nametags.

Explain the rules for making words. This can be simply read from one of the scoring sheets (see below). Players are responsible for keeping track of their scores. There will be two winners, the person who scores the most points and the person who comes up with the single word that's worth the most points.

Decide on a time limit, announce it, and give the signal to begin.

DURING THE GAME: Watch for lost souls. Make sure everyone understands what they're supposed to be doing. Stress the rule that prevents players from using the same person more than once.

SCORING: Be sure to have your chosen reference work on hand to check the validity of words.

Find out who has the highest scoring word by using the process of elimination. First players with a word worth more than 50 points raise their hands, then more than 60, more than 70, etc. Continue until there's only one person with a raised hand. You could have a tie.

Ask the winner(s) to come up to the front of the room or the stage. They will now call out the names of the people in their highest-scoring word, one at a time. Those people should come to the front of the room, stand in order, and say their letters aloud. If it's a legal word and the score is valid, you have one of your two winners.

The total-points winner will take a little time to determine. Ask everyone to write their total points on their scoring sheet and hand them in. Find the sheet with the highest score and check the validity of the words and the scores. Keep checking until you have a legal highest score.

Scoring Sheet for Peobble

You're trying to arrange the letters other people are wearing into the highest-scoring words.

Scrabble rules: All words labeled as a part of speech (including those listed of foreign origin, and as archaic, obsolete, colloquial, slang, etc.) are allowed except words that are always capitalized, abbreviations, prefixes and suffixes standing alone, and words requiring a hyphen or an apostrophe.

Words score the combined point values of their letters. Using a Double Word Score doubles your score for that word; using a Triple Word Score triples your score for that word.

Peobble rules: Words must have at least three letters and be no longer than seven letters. The name of each player whose letter is used must be included with the word. No one can be used more than once. To score a lot of points, you will need a lot different names. You cannot use more than one Double or Triple Word Score to increase a word's score, but there can be more than one in a word.

Name _____

Word	Score	Word	Score
_____	_____	_____	_____
_____	_____	_____	_____
_____	_____	_____	_____
_____	_____	_____	_____
_____	_____	_____	_____
_____	_____	_____	_____
_____	_____	_____	_____
_____	_____	_____	_____
_____	_____	_____	_____
_____	_____	_____	_____
_____	_____	_____	_____
_____	_____	_____	_____

Total _____   Total _____

TOTAL POINTS _____

Letter Heads

by Charles Goldstein (Tilegod)

Category: mixer/cooperative
Players: 25–100+ and one emcee
Playing time: 15–30 minutes
Materials: 3" × 5" cards, tape/elastic bands, oaktag, markers

This is a challenging mixer for groups that are good at organizing themselves and talented at words and puzzles.

PREPARATION: For this game to work most elegantly, determine exactly how many people will be playing. You'll need that many 3" × 5" cards and some way to attach them to people's foreheads. One good way is to use sewing elastic to make headbands in small, medium, and large sizes. (Alternatively, you can ask people to tape the cards to each other's backs, but we prefer the bands.)

Find a quote, quip, lyric, or joke that has the same number of letters, multiplied by three, as the number of players. For example, with 50

players you'll need a quote that contains 150 letters. The easiest way to do this is with a word processor that can count the number of characters in a highlighted section. (Remove the punctuation: these programs count *characters*, not letters.) If a quote doesn't have the right number of letters, try rewording it. This is not recommended for classic or very well-known quotes: "To be or not, that is a question," is not to be!

Try to find a quote that's appropriate for the occasion, date, location, or group. For example "Come on along and listen to the lullaby of Broadway," might be good for a convention in New York City.

Having decided on a quote, eliminate the punctuation and spaces, divide it into trigrams, which are groups of three consecutive letters, and write one trigram on each 3" × 5" card. It will look something like this: ITW ILL LOO KSO MET HIN GLI KET HIS. Write the trigrams large enough to be seen from a few feet away. (You can make the game a little easier by writing all the trigrams from the same sentences on cards of the same color. If the group is having trouble solving, tell them about the color-coding to move things along.)

Now write out the quote's enumeration. This is the number of letters in each word, in order, with punctuation. For example, our New York quote would have this enumeration: 4 2 5 3 6 2 3 7 2 *8. Asterisks denote proper nouns. During the game this enumeration should be displayed on a large poster, blackboard, or easel, so that players can refer to it while solving.

BEFORE THE GAME: Shuffle the cards and hand them out, facedown, to each player. If you have place settings, you can distribute the cards in advance at each place. In either case, make sure to tell the players not to look at their cards. Also make sure each table has enough tape or headbands.

INSTRUCTIONS: This game is an exercise in cooperation. Players put their headbands on and insert in them their index cards with the printed side facing out so that all the letters are readable.

Explain that the letters are parts of a quote with the spaces and punctuation removed and with the letters split into three-letter groups. The enumeration of the quote (explain "enumeration," as above) is on the blackboard (or whatever you're using). The players' job is to arrange themselves so that the letters on their heads spell out the quote.

Players may not ask or tell what is on their own or anyone else's head. The only way they can arrange themselves is to help each other move to the proper place. Set a time limit.

DURING THE GAME: Watch for lost souls. Make sure that people understand what they're supposed to be doing. If they seem to be having a hard time, give them clues. For example, you can let them in on the color-coding of the sentences or give them one or two words in the quote by writing them in under their numbers in the enumeration.

AFTER THE GAME: If the group has managed to arrange themselves correctly, announce their success and read out the quote.

Noah's Ark

by John Chaneski

Category: mixer
Players: 30–100+ and one emcee
Playing time: 10–20 minutes
Materials: index cards

This mixer should be reserved for youngsters (or grownups who like to act like youngsters). Each player is given an index card on which is written the name of an animal. They're job is to locate the one other player in the room who has the same animal. The catch? *No talking.* Players have to act like the animal and ferret out their mate. (Sorry.)

PREPARATION: On pairs of index cards, write the names of various animals. Try to keep the types of creatures varied to avoid confusion. Naturally, the smaller your group, the easier it is to come up with suitably varied species. Try to think of animals that make unique sounds, move in unique ways or both. Here are some suggestions:

Bear	Duck	Lion
Canary	Elephant	Mouse
Cat	Flamingo	Owl
Chicken	Frog	Pig
Chimpanzee	Gazelle	Pigeon
Cow	Gorilla	Rabbit
Crab	Hippo	Snake
Dog	Horse	Wolf

BEFORE THE GAME: Mix up the cards and give one to each player. Instruct them not to look at what's on the card until the signal is given. If your group is made up of an equal number of boys and girls or men and women and you feel it is not inappropriate, you can play up the "Noah's Ark" angle by giving every male animal a matching female.

INSTRUCTIONS: Each player "is" the animal on his or her card and must find its brother, sister, or mate. Since animals can't speak, players have to move around, make noises, and generally act like the animals they are!

When two matching animals think they've found each other, they still may not refer to their cards but instead they hop, crawl, skitter, or gallop over to Noah (that's you) to register the union. (You may want to offer a small prize.) If they don't match, send them back into the wild to keep searching.

DURING THE GAME: Your job is to determine valid matches. You can either remain in place and have the animals come to you, or wander around. If you wander, you might want to coach stray players that don't seem to be imitating their animals too well.

WINNERS: Noah's Ark is best as a very informal mixer designed to get people up and moving about rather than to determine winners. If you simply must have winners, pick the animal pair that comes together soonest.

Zoo Escape

This variation on Noah's Ark can be useful for sorting people into teams or handling a super-large group. Say you need to sort 100 people into teams of four. Write the same type of animal on four index cards. Instruct the players that they are to track down the other members of their herd, pack, pride, flock, school, etc.

Action-Reaction

by John Chaneski

Category: mixer
Players: 30–100+ and one emcee
Playing time: 10–20 minutes
Materials: index cards

Another good mixer, Action-Reaction also works well with a gregarious group. Players are once again looking for their match in a crowd, but this time most players will be doing something other than what their intended partner is doing.

PREPARATION: On pairs of index cards, write out various actions that people can perform upon, to, or toward another person, and also write that action's effect on the other person. For example, one card might say, "Tickle," while its corresponding pair would say, "Being tickled." Be as wild and creative as you like.

Here are a few more examples:

Action	Reaction
Scratching someone's back	Having your back scratched
Reading someone's palm	Having your palm read
Giving a manicure	Getting a manicure
Goosing someone	Getting goosed
Telling a secret	Hearing a secret
Giving a back rub	Getting a back rub
Drilling a tooth	Having a tooth drilled
Giving a shave	Getting a shave
Arresting someone	Getting arrested
Feeding the baby	Getting fed baby food
Giving a museum tour	Listening to a museum tour guide
Dealing Three Card Monte	Getting taken at Three Card Monte
Taking a picture	Having your picture taken
Painting a portrait	Having your portrait painted
Fainting	Catching someone who's fainting

To make things clear, you might indicate on the cards whether the player is performing an action or a reaction. For example: "Action: Testing someone's reflexes," and "Reaction: Having your reflexes tested."

34

Some actions and reactions might be identical, with both people cooperating at the same action. For example:

Using a two-man saw
Shaking hands
Hugging someone
Fencing
Having a shootout
Waltzing
Playing peekaboo
Giving a high five

When the cards are prepared, keep the pairs together. Don't mix them up before you know exactly how many people will be playing.

BEFORE THE GAME: Count the players and make sure you have exactly half as many pairs of action-reaction cards as players. Now mix up the cards and distribute them. Instruct players not to read what's on their card until the signal is given.

INSTRUCTIONS: Each card contains either an action or a reaction to it. At your signal, players put their cards away and begin performing either the action or reaction. No talking is allowed. If an action or reaction has a stopping point, players should perform it repeatedly.

On your second signal, players begin making their way around the room (continuing to perform, of course), trying to find the one other player who is performing the matching action or reaction. When two people think they've found each other, they go to you to confirm the fact.

DURING THE GAME: As in Noah's Ark, you can either stay in one easily accessible location to judge the pairs or wander around and offer assistance while you judge.

WINNERS: Like Noah's Ark, this game works best as an informal mixer, but if you must have a winner, you can reward the first pair to find each other. You could also judge the teams on their acting-reacting ability and declare a winner among the best actors.

Duplicate Wurdz

by Thomas Weisswange (Al DeSuda)

Category: word/teams (or individual)
Players: 12–100+ and one emcee
Playing time: about 5 minutes per team
Materials: One complete set of Scrabble tiles for each 12 players, pens/pencils, one scoresheet per team, one scoring sheet for the emcee, a timer, a standard reference work for settling disputes

In Duplicate Bridge, teams take turns playing each other's hands, and the winner is the team that scored the best with the same hands that everyone has played. Duplicate Wurdz is similar, but it's a word game and much easier to learn.

PREPARATION: Not much. Estimate how many players there will be so you can arrange for the appropriate number of tiles. You can ask players to bring their own sets (make sure they're returned complete and undamaged!), or buy enough Scrabble sets yourself. These can be awarded to the top two or three teams as prizes or donated to charity.

If it isn't possible to acquire Scrabble sets, you can make your own tiles from scrap wood, cardboard, or old playing cards. Use the letter frequency chart from a Scrabble game as a guide.

Each table will require a pen or pencil and a scoresheet like the one on page 38. Decide in advance which reference work or works to use as your standard for qualifying words. We suggest *Merriam-Webster's Collegiate Dictionary* together with *The Official Scrabble Players Dictionary*. The latter, though it contains more obscure words, includes no words longer than eight letters.

BEFORE THE GAME: Group the players into roughly equal teams of three or four at each table. Number the teams and make sure each has a scoresheet and a pencil. Ask one member of each team to blindly choose 25 letter tiles and place them facedown on the table. Once everyone has done this, begin the instructions.

INSTRUCTIONS: When the referee gives the signal, each team turns its 25 tiles faceup. Teams then have three minutes to arrange those letters into words. Scrabble rules apply as to permitted words, except for length. That is, all words labeled as a part of speech (including those listed of foreign origin, and as archaic, obsolete, colloquial, slang, etc.) are allowed except words that are always capitalized, abbreviations, prefixes and suffixes standing alone, and words requiring a hyphen or an apostrophe. Words must be at least three letters long and must appear in the reference works being used.

When the three minutes are up, it's time to score the words. Each team writes its assigned number in the space provided on the scoresheet and enters the words in the spaces next to it and the score for that set of tiles. Words are scored according to the square of their length; that is, a three-letter word scores 9 points, a four-letter word 16 points, and so on. A table at the top of each scoresheet will help with the scoring. One last thing about scoring: Each letter not used in a word takes 20 points away from that team's score!

When the scoring is finished, teams leave their letter tiles faceup, mix them, place their scoresheets facedown on top of them, then move to the next table. When everyone is settled, the referee gives a signal to remove the scoresheets and reveal the tiles beneath them. Teams then have three minutes to rearrange those new letters into words as before.

Every team will eventually work on every set of letters, trying to get a higher score on each set than every other team. Each team outscored is worth one point; each team tied, half a point. The team with the highest overall score wins.

RUNNING THE GAME: Organize the movement of teams from table to table. Walk them through each step of the game. Remind them not to turn over the scoresheets when they get to a new table and explain how to fill out those sheets at the end of each round. When each team has worked every set of tiles, collect the scoresheets and determine the winners. (Let someone else collect the tiles—you're doing enough work!)

KEEP IN MIND: If a team uses an illegal word, each letter in that word counts as an unused word and costs the team 20 points. If you need to return the tile sets back to their original owners, keep a close eye on how the letters are distributed and collected.

Scoring Table

Letters	Score		Letters	Score
3	9		11	121
4	16		12	144
5	25		13	169
6	36		14	196
7	49		15	225
8	64		16	256
9	81		17	289
10	100		18	324

Duplicate Wurdz Scoresheet

Letters _____

Team #	Wurdz	Score
_____	_____	_____
_____	_____	_____
_____	_____	_____
_____	_____	_____
_____	_____	_____
_____	_____	_____
_____	_____	_____

Set a Spell

by Fraser Simpson (Fraz)

Category: word/individuals
Players: 20–100+ and one emcee
Playing time: 45+ minutes
Materials: paper, pens/pencils, oaktag, markers,
metronome (optional)

Set a Spell can be played by groups of just about any age level. It consists of two parts. Although you can play either part by itself, it works best as a combined challenge.

PREPARATION: For part one, you'll need a list of commonly misspelled words or words that are usually heard rather than read. *The World Almanac and Book of Facts* contains lists of commonly misspelled words and words used in the previous year's National Spelling Bee. Create a reference sheet with about 25 words along with their definitions and a sentence illustrating how each of them is used.

For part two, you'll need 50 strips of oaktag measuring about 3" × 24" each. On 10 of them, use the markers to write 10 five-letter words chosen from your reference sheet. These words don't have to be particularly hard to spell, but they shouldn't be too easy, either. On another 10 strips write 10 six-letter words, 10 seven-letter words on 10 other strips, 10 eight-letter words on 10 others, and 10 nine-letter words on the last 10 strips.

BEFORE THE GAME: Make sure each player has a piece of paper and a pen or pencil.

INSTRUCTIONS: This is a little spelling test. Players write down 20 words that you read aloud, allowing 15 seconds for each word. Make sure no one is cheating! When everyone is finished, they all trade papers with their neighbors. Players now "grade" their neighbor's spelling while you read aloud the correct spellings.

When you're done, players reclaim their papers. Ask those who got more than 10 right to raise their hands. Then ask those with 11 or more right to do the same. Continue in this way until you see which players did best. Ask the top 12 players to go to the front of the room and stand side by side facing the group. Then give the instructions for part two (see next game).

Spelling eeB

by Henry Picciotto (Hot)

This is like a classic spelling bee but with a twist.

INSTRUCTIONS: Begin by giving the first person a five-letter word to spell. Remember that in a spelling bee, you must say the word, spell it, and then repeat it; for example, "rhythm, r-h-y-t-h-m, rhythm." If the first person spells it correctly, give the second player a new word. If any player fails to spell a word correctly, that player drops out and the next player gets to try the same word.

To keep things even among the players, the rest of the group can keep time while each speller speaks and spells on the beat. You can use the metronome to keep time here. If you don't, make sure the group's clapping doesn't speed up, as it tends to do. Display the word, on the oaktag, to the rest of the group as players attempt to spell it.

After each player has had a chance to spell a five-letter word, switch to high gear and make things a little more challenging. This time give each player a six-letter word, but here's the twist: the words have to be spelled backward. As the game proceeds, you'll advance to seven-letter words, eight-letter words, and so on—all words longer than five letters are to be delleps drawkcab!—until only one player is left. That player is the winner. If you run out of words before a winner is determined, you can declare two people co-champions.

KEEP IN MIND: Words that sound similar can be confusing. Make sure the group knows you said "deceive" and not "receive," for example.

Small Talk

by Scott Marley (Hudu)

Category: trivia/team
Players: 12–50 and one emcee
Playing time: 1–1½ hours
Materials: newsprint or other large pieces of paper or cardboard, markers

Like Chain Reaction, this game challenges players to think quickly and accurately. And like Two-Player Chain Reaction, it's played by teams of two. You can match people randomly or with suitable partners, or you can let them choose up teams on their own.

The big difference in Small Talk is that the clue-giver works alone and can use only one-syllable words. For example, if the target word is "ballet" the clue-giver could say, "This is a kind of dance where girls and boys go up on their toes as in *Swan Lake*." Each team has one minute to get as many target words as possible. The guesser can guess as often as he likes with no penalty for wrong guesses.

PREPARATION: You'll need paper or cards with answers printed on them that can be seen by everyone in the room. These answers should be people, places, and things that everyone will recognize immediately.

RUNNING THE GAME: This game is a little harder than it sounds. If the clue-giver tries to talk too fast, he'll invariably use two-syllable (or longer!) words. The audience is in charge of catching those mistakes. If a clue-giver uses a word of more than one syllable, the target word is forfeited and the team must move on to the next one. The clue-giver can pass as often as he likes. You might want to advise the clue-givers to go slowly at first.

WINNERS: The team that gets the most correct answers in one minute wins. If time allows, you might want to have a playoff round among the top five or top three teams.

Small Talk Mixer

by Dean Howard (Shrdlu)

Category: mixer/word
Players: 12–50+ and one emcee
Playing time: 30–60 minutes
Materials: oaktag, markers, tape, dot stickers, cards numbered from 1 to the number of players

Another version of Small Talk. Preparation is very similar to the game Word Chain (page 22). You can play it competitively or, omitting the colored dots and numbered cards, noncompetitively.

PREPARATION: For each player, write a goal answer on individual oaktag cards measuring about 5" × 7". The words don't have to be very large, but should be easily legible from about three feet away. As in Small Talk, these answers should be immediately recognizable people, places, and things. You'll also need sheets of dot stickers of any bright color. Each player will need at least 50 dots.

When you're ready to begin, you can either hand one card face-down to each player or, if you're using place settings, place a card at each setting ahead of time. In either case, remind the players not to look at their cards. Also make sure that each table has enough tape of some kind so that players can tape the cards to one another. Give out the stickers, too, but keep the numbered cards with you.

INSTRUCTIONS: Every player has a card with a word or short phrase on it. This card is to be taped to the back of the player on the right, without letting that player see what's on the card. When everyone is wearing a card, continue with the instructions.

The word on each card represents a well-known person, place, or thing. Players must not be told what's on their backs—the object is for them to figure that out by asking other players questions. Each player may ask any other player only one question, so everyone will have to do a lot of mixing to get enough information. There's a penalty for asking more than one question: the player who is asked sticks a colored dot on the player who violated the rule. These dots reduce the player's score.

Here's the catch: When asking a question or giving an answer, only one-syllable words are allowed! Example: If the target word is "Chicago," a question might be "Is my word a place?" and the answer might be "Yes, a big place where the wind blows." If either player breaks the one-syllable rule, that player gets a sticker from the other one. An answer that would break the rule: "Yes, it's a big city."

A player who has figured out his or her word goes to the front of the room, takes a numbered card (which are taken in numerical order), and tells the emcee the word. If it's wrong, the emcee takes back the number and the player goes back to try again. If the word is correct, the chosen number is added to the number of stickers that player has received, and that's the player's final score. The player with the lowest score is the winner.

After a certain amount of time (announced before play begins) the game ends.

SCORING: Keep track of the correct players by writing their names and scores on the back of the numbered card. You might consider awarding second and third place.

KEEP IN MIND: At various times during the game, remind everyone of the one-syllable rule. Make sure the dots that players are sticking on others come from their sheet of dots and are not the dots that others have stuck on them! Players may not remove their stickers! One way to prevent this subterfuge is to have the players place the dots on each other's backs, perhaps on the answer card itself if you have left enough room around or next to the answer.

NONCOMPETITIVE VARIATION: Omit the dot stickers and the numbered cards and don't bother with scoring. Just play for the fun of it.

Dictum

by Charles Goldstein

Category: word/individual (or teams)
Players: 12–100+ and one emcee
Playing time: 30–60 minutes
Materials: photocopies of handouts

This is for word lovers. To make the game more challenging, players can play as individuals within a brief time limit, or they can compete as collaborative two-person teams with a more generous time allowance.

Players are given a list of keywords. For each one they must try to come up with the word or phrase that most closely follows it in the dictionary. ("Dictum" immediately follows "dictionary" in the dictionary we recommend.) Like some of our other favorite games, this one doesn't require precise answers but awards points for answers that come close. The closer the answer is to the correct one, the more points it earns.

PREPARATION: Create a list of 10 to 20 keywords, or more if you prefer. Decide on a standard dictionary. I recommend *Merriam-Webster's Collegiate Dictionary, Tenth Edition.* Make enough copies of the list for every player.

INSTRUCTIONS: In front of every player is a list of keywords. For each of them, players try to think of a word that closely follows it in the dictionary. The closer the player's word to the keyword, the more points it scores.

RUNNING THE GAME: There's nothing much for you to do during play except to make sure no one is cheating. Instead of passing out the list of keywords, you can read them aloud, one at a time. Though this is a more "active" method, be sure to give everyone plenty of time to think before you say the next keyword.

Here are some examples of Dictum words and lists:

	Main Street	**dragoon**	**stumpy**
10	maintain	drag queen	stun
9	maintenance	drag race	stung
8	maintop	dragster	stun gun
7	main-topmast	drag strip	stunk
6	main yard	drain	stunner
5	mair	drainage	stunning
4	maisonette	drainpipe	stunt
3	maître d'	Draize test	stuntman
2	maître d'hôtel	drake	stuntwoman
1	maize	dram	stupa

SCORING: To build suspense, give the answers in reverse order. A player whose answer is closest to the actual entry that follows the keyword in the dictionary scores 10 points. The next closest scores 9 points, the next 8 points, and so on. No points are scored for any answer more than 10 entries away.

To illustrate, you can use the keyword "Main Street." Players who wrote "maize" score one point. Whoever wrote "maître d'hôtel" earns 2 points, and so on. When you've completed the scoring, determine who has the most points by the process of elimination, as described earlier.

Yoga Instruction Dictum
by Dean Howard

Category: word/trivia/teams/
individuals/noncompetitive

This variation on Dictum is a bit tougher and is usually played non-competitively. If you try it competitively, you can add to the fun by awarding "style points" for particularly clever or amusing answers. This is a pretty subjective area, so you should use them only to make your games more enjoyable.

The idea is to give players a category from the local yellow pages and ask them to come up with the next closest category alphabetically. In my local yellow pages, "Yoga Instruction" would immediately follow "Yellow Pages." If yours is different, feel free to call the game whatever you like.

To make the categories more gettable, you can ignore subcategories such as those ending with the word "Retail," "Wholesale," "Repairing," etc. Just don't forget to inform your players that you're doing this.

Here are a few sample categories and lists from my local phone book:

Organs—Tuning and Repairing
10	Oriental Goods—Retail
9	Oriental Goods—Wholesale & Manufacturers
8	Ornamental Metal Work
7	Orthodontists
6	Orthopedic Appliances
5	Osteopathic Physicians
4	Outboard Motors
3	Oxygen
2	Oxygen Therapy Equipment
1	Package Designing & Development

Copying Machine—Sales, Service & Supplies

10 Copyright Service

9 Core Borings

8 Corn Products

7 Corsets & Girdles

6 Cosmetics & Perfumes—Retail

5 Cosmetics & Toilet Preparations—Wholesale & Manufacturers

4 Cosmetology Schools

3 Costumes—Masquerade & Theatrical

2 Counseling—Personal & Family

1 Counselors—Human Relations

Group Therapy

10 Guard Dogs

9 Guard & Patrol Services

8 Guards—Door & Window

7 Guest Houses

6 Guns & Gunsmiths

5 Gutters & Downspouts

4 Gymnasiums

3 Gymnasiums—Equipment & Supplies

2 Gymnastics Instruction

1 Hair Cutting

Life Sentences

by Francis Heaney (Lunch Boy)

Category: word/mixer/teams/creative
Players: 12–50+ and one emcee
Playing time: 15–30 minutes
Materials: pencils/pens, paper

Life Sentences is a kind of mixer; in fact, what your players will be doing is mixing themselves! It can last as long or as (sadistically) short as you like.

PREPARATION: This game is simple for you, but difficult for the players! All you need to do beforehand is to make sure there's enough paper and pencils for everyone. Before the game begins, arrange your players into teams of 4 to 8, depending on how many are playing. You may want to number the tables to differentiate the teams. We'll assume that you have each team seated at a different table.

INSTRUCTIONS: The team at each table writes down all the team members' names. Use first names only for a challenging game; add last names for an easier one. Each team must now compose a sentence or two (or three) made up of the scrambled letters of the team members' names.

Allow 15 minutes (half an hour for an easier game). Players may work individually or together.

DURING THE GAME: See how people are doing. If it's slow going, give them extra time. Announce how much time is left every 10 minutes or so and when only one minute remains. When time has run out, ask one person from each team to bring the team's sentence(s) to you at the front of the room, written on the page with the team members' names.

SCORING: You can do this very informally by simply reading off the teams' sentences one at a time. Or you can ask the group to applaud for sentences that they think are particularly well constructed or amusing. Narrow it down to three and then read those again to determine a winner. You will have to take some time to make sure that the sentences contain all the letters in the team's names and no extra letters. This is only fair, if you are going to declare winners.

Squares
Traditional

Category: word/individuals
Players: 12–100+ and one emcee
Playing time: 30–60 minutes
Materials: paper, pens/pencils, reference books

What's great about Squares is that it's simple to run and simple to explain, and it can be played in several different ways (see the variations below). Also, every player can affect the game in some way. Once everyone understands the game, it can move rather quickly, so you can play two or three games in a relatively brief period.

PREPARATION: Print some sheets like the one on page 54, which basically consists of a 5 × 5 grid and spaces to enter scores. You'll need at least one for every player, more if you want to play several games.

You might want a larger or rectangular grid for more players. For example, a 5 × 7 grid works perfectly for 35 players. Distribute these sheets to the players before the game.

INSTRUCTIONS: The object is for each player to form a sort of crossword in the grid provided, making as many words as possible across or down. For a more challenging game, include both left-to-right corner-to-corner diagonals in the scoring. You can also add the rule that only the longest word in each row, column, or diagonal scores points.

Ask someone to say a letter, any letter.

Players immediately enter that letter anywhere they like in their grid. Once entered, a letter stays put. Someone else now announces a second letter, and players enter that letter as before. Continue until 25 letters have been called and all grids are completely filled. (More than 25 letters will be needed to fill grids larger than 5 × 5, of course.)

The words are then scored. Every word at least two letters long (even if it's part of another word) earns points equal to the number of letters in that word. For example, a four-letter word, even if it's part of another word, earns 4 points; every five-letter word earns 5 points, and so on. The player with the most points is the winner.

Here's a sample finished grid and how it is scored:

Score

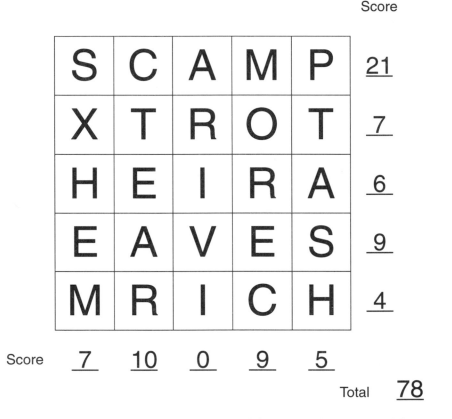

					Score
S	C	A	M	P	21
X	T	R	O	T	7
H	E	I	R	A	6
E	A	V	E	S	9
M	R	I	C	H	4

Score 7 10 0 9 5

Total **78**

Across: SCAM (4), CAMP (4), CAM (3), AMP (3), SCAMP (5), AM (2), TROT (4), ROT (3), HEIR (4), HE (2), EAVE (4), EAVES (5), RICH (4)

Down: HE (2), EM (2), HEM (3), TEA (3), TEAR (4), EAR (3), MORE (4), OR (2), ORE (3), ASH (3), AS (2)

Total Score: 78 points

DURING THE GAME: When deciding who calls out letters, pick names from a hat or use some other system that gives everyone a chance. Make sure the order is random. If you're playing with fewer than 25 players, some of them will get to call out a letter more than once. Some people play faster than others, but you should make sure everyone has enough time. It's a good idea to call a five-second warning before moving on to the next name. Keep track of which letters have been called so that if there's a problem you can check the winner's grid later.

One fun aspect of Squares is that people who call out easy letters, such as E, T, O, A, and N are cheered, and those who call out tough letters like J, Q, X, and Z get booed but enjoy their notoriety anyway!

SCORING: Players score their own grids when they're filled. Determine who has the highest score as described above. Check the validity of that player's grid by calling out the letters in it to make sure they correspond to the letters called. Then go over the player's words and their scores by announcing them. A player could be embarrassed by a mistake, so do the checking out loud only if you think no one's feelings will be hurt.

If you want to award runner-up prizes, check more grids.

KEEP IN MIND: Watch out for people erasing previously filled-in letters. Once a letter is entered, that's where it stays. When checking high-scoring grids, look for signs of erasure!

Square Removal Variation

After the 10th letter has been called, the next player does not choose a letter to go into the grid, but selects one previously called letter to be *removed* from the grid. Do this again after the 20th letter. If you use this rule, players should use pencils with erasers.

Cross-Squares Version, by Henry Picciotto

This version adds variety by introducing a crossword-type element. Cross-Squares is better for larger groups. You should increase the size of the grid to about the number of players. This will usually mean a rectangular grid. For instance, with 150 players the grid would be 10 × 15.

Play proceeds exactly as in regular Squares, with this exception: When called, a player has the option of announcing either a letter or a black square. If a player calls "black square," everyone must immediately place a black square anywhere they like in their grid.

Scoring works the same as in the regular game.

Double-Cross-Squares

This is a variation on Cross-Squares. Players make up teams of two and must trade grids after every seven letters. This version adds the challenge of trying to figure out what the partner is thinking, so no table talk is allowed.

Scoring is the same as in the regular game, but teams earn the points from both grids.

Poker Squares

This variation is for adults who prefer card games and gambling to word games. Poker Squares can be played on 5 × 5 grids only.

Instead of calling out letters, players name standard playing cards. The object is to form 10 five-card poker hands, five horizontally and five vertically. As the moderator, you will have to keep track of cards that have been called by culling them from an actual deck.

SCORING: Once the grids are full, players score points for each valid poker hand according to the following chart.

No pair = 0 points
One pair = 1 point
Two pair = 3 points
Flush = 5 points
Three of a kind = 6 points
Full House = 10 points
Straight = 12 points
Four of a kind = 16 points
Straight flush = 20 points
Royal Flush = 30 points

On the next page is a sample grid.

Across: One pair (1), No pair (0), Straight (12), Full house (10), Three of a kind (6)

Down: Four of a kind (16), One pair (1), No pair (0), One pair (1), Flush (5)

Total: 52 points

Find the overall winner(s) through the process of elimination.

For variety you might wish to include two Wild Jokers in your deck and allow them to be called. Instead of having players call out cards, you may want to draw them from a deck at random. While this reduces player interaction and strategy, it increases the luck factor and adds suspense.

					Score
A♥	4♣	7♥	K♥	7♦	1
A♠	J♠	9♦	5♣	2♦	0
A♣	4♥	2♣	3♣	5♦	12
10♥	10♣	6♠	6♥	6♦	10
A♦	Q♦	3♥	3♠	3♦	6
Score 16	1	0	1	5	

Total 52

Squares Game Sheet

SCORING: word score = # of letters in word

All words labeled as a part of speech (including those listed of foreign origin, and as archaic, obsolete, colloquial, slang, etc.) are allowed except words that are always capitalized, abbreviations, prefixes and suffixes standing alone, and words requiring a hyphen or an apostrophe.

Score

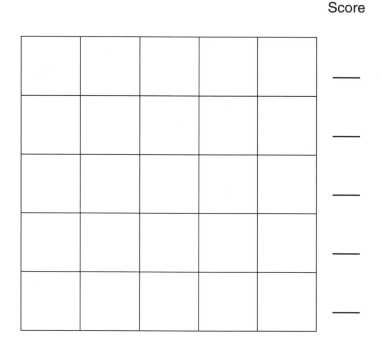

Score —   —   —   —   —

Total   —

Dictionary Race

by Scott Marley

Category: word/trivia/individuals (or teams)
Players: 12–100+ and one emcee
Playing time: 20–30 minutes
Materials: Scrabble tile set with bag, instruction sheet, writing materials

This race goes not to the swift but to the smart. You can play this game as a timed event to make it really challenging, but the regular version is great.

PREPARATION: The rules might be a little confusing to novices, so it's a good idea to have printed instruction sheets available, though it may not be necessary.

Each round requires five categories of various types. Some appear below, but feel free to make up your own. You'll also have to decide on a standard dictionary to be your reference for legal words.

INSTRUCTIONS: This is a race through the dictionary. In each round, draw one letter tile from the bag and announce a category. Players must write down an item in that category beginning with the announced letter, trying to think of the item that appears earliest in alphabetical order. For example, if "C" is chosen and the category is "Fruit," players could write "cranberry." But "coconut," being earlier alphabetically, would be better.

Then announce a second category, still using the same letter. Players must now write down an item that comes alphabetically *after* the first answer but as close to it as possible. Let's say the next category is "Flowers." If the first answer was "cranberry," the second might be "crocus," which closely follows "cranberry" alphabetically. The closest answer a player may be able to recall could take him to the next letter of the alphabet, or beyond. For example, if a player cannot think of "crocus" he might answer "dahlia" or "daisy."

Continue that way through five categories. You may "wrap around" the alphabet; that is, "A" follows "Z."

At the end of the round, the player who traveled the shortest distance to the fifth word wins (in other words, whoever has the alphabetically earlier fifth word wins that round). Ties are broken by comparing the fourth items, and so on.

You can use the following example on your handout, along with the default rules below.

Example: Letter N:
Category 1: A word of at least 6 letters in which vowels and consonants alternate.
Category 2: A body part.
Category 3: A word ending in "Y" but not "LY."
Category 4: Any word alphabetically following the word you just wrote, but not related to it (e.g., "reliable" can't be followed by "reliant").
Category 5: A plant.

Sample answers: NANOMETER, NAPE, NAPERY, NASAL, NASTURTIUM.

Better answers: NAGANA, NAIL, NAIVETY, NAKED, NARCISSUS.

Note that the fifth word of the second set of answers comes earlier in the dictionary than the fifth word of the first set.

If a category requires a word with a certain property, it is assumed to be a non-capitalized, English word. Words must be entries in the chosen dictionary. If the name of a person is required, the last name is to be used. For example, Henry Wallace counts as W.

Ignore leading articles, such as "a," "an," and "the" in titles. For example, *The Lion King* counts as L. If a category is time-sensitive, apply it to the present. For example, if the category is "Members of the Supreme Court," John Marshall would not be a valid answer since he is not currently sitting on the Court.

We recommend playing several games and then pitting the winners of each game against each other in a final round. You could even have a Dictionary Marathon with 10 categories instead of five.

Reference Race
This tough variation is for groups with a particular interest. Instead of using a dictionary, you could use one of the subject-specific books below or one of your own. Though you'll have to come up with categories that fit the specific subject, we've included a few to get you started.

Remember that the criteria for an answer will vary according to the way each book lists information. For example, *The Billboard Book of Top 40 Hits* lists performers and groups with the songs of each listed below their entry and then lists songs alphabetically. You could use just performers, performers and songs combined (ignoring the alphabetized list), or just songs.

This version is very difficult unless your group really knows their stuff!

Suggested Specialized Reference Books

Leonard Maltin's Movie & Video Guide
Categories
1. A one-word title
2. A movie with a man's name in its title
3. A black and white movie
4. A foreign film
5. An Oscar winner

The Billboard Book of Top 40 Hits
Categories
1. An all-male group
2. A song with a woman's name in the title
3. A Grammy winner
4. A performer married to another performer
5. An instrumental hit

The Baseball Encyclopedia
Categories
1. A shortstop
2. A player who had at least a .300 career average
3. A Hall-of-Famer
4. A player whose first and last initials are the same
5. A player who played in two or more World Series

The Complete Directory to Prime Time Network and Cable TV Shows
Categories
1. A western
2. A title that begins and ends with the same consonant
3. A title that contains an adjective
4. A show that did not last more than a season
5. A current show

News Clips
by Will Shortz (WILLz)

Category: word/teams
Players: 12–100+ and one emcees
Playing time: 30–60 minutes
Materials: instruction sheet, pens/pencils, tape, newspapers

This is a kind of scavenger hunt. The object is to find particular words and sentences in a newspaper. One of its best features is that it gets nearly everyone involved nearly all of the time. It can be a strictly timed competition, with the amount of time allotted up to you, or a group exercise just for fun.

PREPARATION: Have enough instruction sheets printed up for your entire group. They'll be referring to the goals on the sheet throughout the game. You'll need a *lot* of newspapers, so start saving them well ahead of time! You'll need, at the very least, one newspaper for each player, maybe more. The larger the stack, and the more variety among the papers, the better. Make sure you have a place to store the papers before the game and a way of getting them to the game site.

There are several ways to collect 100, 200, 300, or more newspapers. One way is to pick up stacks that people have left out on recycling day before they're collected. You can ask your players to save up and bring a week's worth of newspapers with them. Or you can ask a local paper to donate back issues.

BEFORE THE GAME: Arrange your group into teams of three, four, or five, one team at each table. Ask them to gather several newspapers from your collection. Encourage them to take a few extras and to select different newspapers and those with different dates. Hand out the instruction sheet.

INSTRUCTIONS: The instruction sheets list several items (how many depends on how much time you want the game to take) that players will be searching for in the newspapers. For example, if the first item is "a palindromic word," players will search through their papers for a word that reads the same in both directions (like "madam"). Each item is worth a different number of points, depending on how rare it is. The words or sentences can come from anywhere in the newspaper: headlines, text, cartoons, captions, whatever.

When a team finds an item, they cut it out of the paper. All the collected items will later be taped to a blank sheet of paper and handed in. Remind players to write their names on the sheet. The first team that hands in a complete set wins the game.

DURING THE GAME: There's nothing for you to do. Go grab a soda.

When the first team comes to you with their answers, note the time and check the answers. When you've determined the first-place winner, you can wait for the second- and third-place teams to roll in or you can just announce first place. Be sure to announce how long it took the winning team to complete the search, especially if there are multiple winners. If no team gets all the items when time runs out, the team with the most points for found items wins.

Below is a list of sample goals for the News Clips game. Feel free to be creative and come up with your own.

1. A word of at least 7 letters that alternates consonants and vowels (e.g., bananas). [5 points]

2. Two words in the same paragraph that are anagrams of each other (e.g., rate, tear). [5]

3. A word starting with a silent P. [10]

4. A word of 5 or more letters that starts and ends with the same pair of letters (e.g., church). [10]

5. Two words of 4 or more letters that are the same except for their initial letter (e.g., auction/suction). [10]

6. Two words of 4 or more letters that are reversals of each other (e.g., emit/time). [10]

7. Two words that are homophones but have a different number of letters (e.g., eight/ate). [10]

8. A word of 5 or more letters that is palindromic (e.g., civic). [15]

9. A word of 6 or more letters all of which appear in the first half of the alphabet (e.g., blackmail). [15]

10. A word that has at least 5 letters the same (e.g., possesses). [15]

11. A word that is pronounced like two letters of the alphabet (e.g., envy: N-V). [15]

12. A word of 9 or more letters that contains only one of the 5 vowels, and no Y (e.g., indistinct). [15]

13. Two words of 7 or more letters that are anagrams (e.g., traipse/pirates). [20]

14. A sentence of 5 or more words that does not contain the letter E. [25]

15. Four or more consecutive paragraphs in a single article in which the initial letters of each paragraph spell a common English word. [25]

16. A paragraph that contains every letter of the alphabet. [40]

Transdeletion Twins

by Jim Propp

Category: word/teams/creative
Players: 20–100+ and one emcee
Playing time: 1–2 hours
Materials: hat, pens/pencils, paper

Here's another chance for players to challenge each other one-on-one, including the emcee. This is a game that the players create for each other. A "transdeletion" results from deleting a letter from a word and anagramming the remaining letters into another word. For example, NOT is a transdeletion of INTO; SMOKE is a transdeletion of ESKIMO; and TROUGHS is a transdeletion of ROUGHEST.

PREPARATION: Get a hat. Okay, you don't really need a hat, but you will need something like a bucket or a box. That's all.

BEFORE THE GAME: Ask players to pair off. Make sure everyone has a few sheets of paper and something to write with.

INSTRUCTIONS: Each two-person team is going to create a pair of transdeletion twins for everyone else to solve. Explain what a transdeletion is; using the explanation and examples above. Be sure to point out that the transdeletions are the solving phase of the game and must first be created.

Transdeletion twins are made from a pair of words that normally go together as a common phrase when joined by "and," "but," or "or." For example, using the phrase "SINK or SWIM," one player might add "L" to "SINK" and rearrange the letters to make "KILNS." That player's partner might add "H" to "SWIM" and rearrange the letters to make "WHIMS."

Players collaborate secretly to choose a pair of words to work on and decide who will work on which word. The partners then separate and work independently. When they're done, they hand you three pieces of paper, one with the first new word on it, another with the second new word, and the third with the answer phrase. Players' names must be included, of course.

Drop the single words—but not the answers—into the hat and mix them up. Keep the answer phrases secret and separate.

Now it's time to solve. Draw words randomly from the hat one at a time and read them aloud as the players write them down.

When they've all been read and recorded, players try to discover the original pairs that were used to make the transdeletions. One point is awarded for every pair found. Any unintended pairs that are found are also valid.

As you read the words, make sure everyone hears them correctly. If you are playing yourself, ask someone to make an extra list of words while you are reading. When you've finished reading, begin solving.

SCORING: When the time set aside for solving has elapsed, or when everyone feels they've solved as many as they can, start scoring. Read the pairs from the answer papers that the teams gave you earlier.

When you've gone through all the pairs, ask if anyone has found a pair that was not announced. The group as a whole should decide if a found pair is a valid score.

Find the winners through the process of elimination, as previously described.

Counting Bee
by Henry Picciotto

Category: word/individuals
Players: 12–100+ and one emcee
Playing time: 45+ minutes
Materials: none

This is a simple game, easy to prepare, easy to run, and easy to play. It's difficult only when your opponent is faster than you are! This version is similar to Beat the Champ (page 90).

PREPARATION: You'll need about twice as many words as players. List them on a notepad followed, in parentheses, by the number of letters in each word. This will help the game run smoother and quicker. Words should be at least five letters long. There is no maximum. Try to use words that are interesting and that resist easy counting. Don't use homophones, like "where" and "wear," or words that are easily confused with other words.

BEFORE THE GAME: Divide the group into two approximately even teams. It'll be easier to run if you put someone else in charge of scoring.

INSTRUCTIONS: This game is like a spelling bee, but with the important difference that players don't have to be good spellers. But they do have to be able to count.

One player from each team stands up and you read one of the words from your list. The first standee to correctly announce the number of letters in that word remains standing and that player's team gets one point. The other player sits down, and two other players from that team stand up. You read another word, and the first of the three standees to correctly announce the number of letters in the word remains standing. This time, the winning players earn a point for each standing player on the opposing team.

SCORING: You can play Counting Bee noncompetitively or score it the same way as Beat the Champ.

ABC-VIP

Author unknown

Category: teams
Players: 12–100+ one emcee
Playing time: 1+ hour
Materials: 3" × 5" cards, markers

This is a variation on the old TV game show *Password*. Pairs of clue-givers try to get their teams to guess the identity of a famous person by giving one-word descriptions ... in alphabetical order.

PREPARATION: You'll need the names of famous people printed individually on index cards. For a single game you'll need one-fourth as many names as there are players (100 players, 25 names). This will give everyone a chance to be on a clue-giving team. Make plenty of extras, in case the group wants to play again.

Make sure players know your criteria for determining fame. We consider a famous person to be anyone, living or dead, past or present, real or fictional, who is known by half of the players. If you include non-human (e.g., cartoon) characters or local celebrities, make sure your players know this.

BEFORE THE GAME: Divide the group into two approximately even teams. We'll call them Team A and Team B. Each team will choose a captain, whose job it will be to give the team's official answer each turn. Decide how many celebrities make up a complete game.

INSTRUCTIONS: Teams try to guess the identity of a famous person from one-word clues. For each celebrity, two players from each team will come to the front of the room to give clues. (If you're playing with a smaller group, you can use one clue-giver at a time for each team.) Let's say the first cluing team is Team A. Discreetly give the name of the celebrity to the two clue-givers from Team A, who quietly confer and announce a one-word clue to the entire audience. The rest of Team A goes into a huddle (not too loudly, since team B will be listening!), and the captain announces the team's answer. If the answer is correct, that team earns a point. If not, the clue-givers from Team B get a chance and the rest of Team B gets to answer. The team that gets the answers goes second for the next name.

Here's the catch: the first clue word must begin with the letter "A," and each subsequent clue word must start with the next letter of the alphabet. For example, if the celebrity is Donald Trump, the first clue might be "affluent." If team A doesn't get it right, then Team B could try "building." If Team B doesn't get the answer, Team A tries again, perhaps with "casino." If Team A then gets it right, Team B goes first with the next celebrity, using a clue starting with a "D." The player who must use an E word can use E or F. The same is true for J/K, Q/R, and U/V. The player who must use a W word can use W, X, Y, or Z.

DURING THE GAME: Get the pairs of clue-givers up on stage or in front of the group expeditiously. Give them their celebrity names and answer any questions they might have. Remind them of the consecutive-letter rule. Keep score.

KEEP IN MIND: Clue-givers that confer too loudly.

SCORING: The game ends after going through all the celebrities on the list. The team with the most points wins. In case of a tie, play one tiebreaker round.

Adverbally

Traditional

Category: team
Players: 12–100+ and one emcee
Playing time: 1–2 hours
Materials: index cards, pens/pencils

This game has been cleverly adapted to work with a large crowd. It's best for players who can act outlandishly, think clearly, and reason intuitively.

PREPARATION: Write one adverb on each index card. Try to use interesting adverbs. Here are just a few we found starting with A:

abruptly	anticlimactically
absentmindedly	antiseptically
accidentally	apprehensively
adorably	ashamedly
affectionately	asymmetrically
aimlessly	audibly
alphabetically	awkwardly

When you have enough, mix them up and you're ready to begin.

BEFORE THE GAME: Divide your players into two teams of approximately equal size. Appoint a scorekeeper or keep score yourself.

INSTRUCTIONS: The object is to figure out in what way a performer is doing something. Choose a team to be the first active team, and choose someone from that team to be the first performer. Give that person an index card on which is written an adverb, such as "softly," "angrily," or maybe something a little more unusual, like "anecdotally" or "benevolently." You and the performer will be the only people who see the adverb on the card. (It may be more fun for the inactive team if they know the adverb the active team is trying to guess. If you let them know the word, make sure no one inadvertently blurts out the answer.)

Once the round begins, anyone on the active team may ask the performer, by raising his or her hand to be recognized by the emcee, to act out a specific task in the manner of the adverb on the card. For example, the performer may be asked to mow the lawn or give directions to the nearest gas station. The performer will perform the requested action in the manner of the adverb, without speaking. It's up to the performer to figure out how to mow a lawn "benevolently" or give directions "suicidally."

A performer who believes there is absolutely no way to perform a requested instruction in the manner of the adverb may pass without penalty.

Anyone on the active team may raise his or her hand at any time and say "Guess" to try naming the adverb. If correct, that team scores one point for every guess made and one point for every action the performer performed to that point. Then the other team becomes the active team. If the guess is incorrect, play continues, but the player who guessed wrong must stand up or move to the side and may not make any more guesses or request any more actions.

HE MAY BE "PERFORMING BRAIN SURGERY" BADLY BUT HE'S PLAYING THE GAME BEAUTIFULLY.

DURING THE GAME: Keep track of time. You don't want the game to go on forever. Keep careful track of the number of guesses and the number of performed actions. When everyone has had a chance to perform, call an end to the game.

SCORING: The team with the lowest score wins. You may also want to award a prize to the performer who does the best job of acting out an adverb.

We Love Fortune

by Barbara Selfridge (Banterweight)

Category: creative/teams
Players: 16–100+ and one emcee
Playing time: 1–1½ hours
Materials: pens/pencils, paper, instruction sheet

Some people balk when asked to be creative, but even they can have fun and be funny when guided through the process. We Love Fortune helps players forget the pressure of creation by distracting them with teamwork and clever restrictions on what they produce. As long as they make some kind of sense, the resulting fortunes are entertaining, interesting, and sometimes surreal!

PREPARATION: Make sure that each table has enough paper and writing utensils, as this game consists totally of writing fortunes. Fortunately for your players, they'll have the following instruction sheet to help them in their work. You can have one copy on each table or, ideally, one for each player:

Happy Production Workers, Unite in Joyous Production Quota Achievement!

The Too-Happy Fortune Cookie Fortune Factory announces new production stan-dards designed to eliminate all disturbing repetitions, satisfying every cookie!

Existing Industry Standards
Fortune cookie sayings fall into one of four categories:
• They describe the recipient.
  Example: "You have a reputation for being straightforward and honest."
• They foretell the future.
  Example: "Your lover will never wish to leave you."
• They advise the recipient.
  Example: "Now is the time to try something new."
• They impart general philosophic knowledge.
  Example: "Fear creates danger and courage dispels it."

Note: The great masters love to imply bad fortune while seeming to impart the opposite—what if you *want* your lover to leave? This irony is optional.

Note also: All fortunes have a mandatory seven-word minimum.

The Joyous Integration of New Production Strategies

1. All Too-Happy Fortune Cookie Fortune Factory workers form four-member production teams. You may choose to work in pairs within your team.
2. Each team shall produce one conforming fortune for each of the new production standards, while maintaining existing industry standards and the seven-word minimum.
3. Once you have a fortune for each of the nine new production standards, you can either rewrite them or begin a second set. Both quality and quantity are revered in the Too Happy Fortune Cookie Fortune Factory.

New Production Standards

1. The fortune alternates between words of one and three syllables.
   Example: Everyone shall benefit from collective truths exposing wrong behavior.
2. The fortune includes at least four double letters.
   Example: Seeking good looks leads you to shallowness.
3. The fortune includes no words containing the letter e.
   Example: Confucius say: Multiply thoughts a thousandfold on MSG trip.
4. Each word of the fortune is the same length.
   Example: Boss says work hard, shut face, make like cool mice.
5. Each word of the fortune is one letter longer than the word before.
   Example: You must solve knotty dilemma, creating universal simplicity.
6. Each word of the fortune is one letter shorter than the word before.
   Example: Something mystical beckons beyond death, life, and TV.
7. Each word of the fortune begins with a vowel.

Example: Eat everything available, even asparagus; angst allows uninhibited engorgement.

8. Each word of the fortune begins with the next letter of the alphabet.
Example: Never open purse quickly, relinquishing silver to useless vices.

9. Each word of the fortune begins with the previous letter of the alphabet.
Example: Screaming religious quotations, prophetic or nihilistic, makes laughter.

RUNNING THE GAME: Divide your group into teams of two to six players. Make sure they understand the rules and give examples of each type of fortune so that the categories are clear. The time limit is flexible, but teams should have at least 30 minutes to construct their entries. Use your judgment to gauge when the game is winding down, when most teams are nearly finished, etc. When the game is over, collect the fortunes. Important: Make sure the teams have put their team name and individual names on the back of the entries.

WINNERS: A judge or judges should determine runners-up and winners in each of the nine production categories. The names of these winners should be read aloud to the group. You might want representatives from the winning teams to come forward and read their own fortunes, if time permits. You might also want to let the group determine the top five or top three fortunes by their applause.

Crisis in Publishing

by Fraser Simpson

Category: creative/teams
Players: 24–100+ players and one "production trafficker"
Playing time: 1–1½ hours
Materials: pens/pencils, paper, instruction sheet

In the 1920s, the Surrealists created a unique game, The Exquisite Corpse, that reflected their practice of producing fantastic or incongruous images by juxtapositions or combinations. That game was the inspiration for Crisis in Publishing. Everybody gets to create and there's little pressure on individual players because there are no wrong answers. Like We Love Fortune, this game often has hilarious results.

PREPARATION: Make sure each table has enough paper and writing utensils. The following instruction sheet is all you need to explain the game to your players. You can have one copy on each table or, ideally, one for each player:

Crisis in Publishing!

The Unlettered Press has just entered a "publish or perish" situation. The company motto has always been, "We Give the Public What It Wants—Nobody Reads Anymore Anyway." But according to our tax preparer, the IRS limits the number of years a company may write off its losses.

To get the most books written the fastest and with the least danger of excessive ego investment, we have divided everyone in the company into eight-member "book teams." Each team will produce eight books *tonight,* following the company Formula as well as the company Process.

The Unlettered Formula Fundamentals

• Begin the book with something about to happen to somebody somewhere.

• Plot and self-revelation are the cornerstones of our novels. Something must happen on every page; inevitably, this should give somebody an insight into him- or herself. For instance, if shot, a character may realize: "I'll never say 'Be still, my heart' again," or, more simply: "I was right: something's afoot!"

- A character's feelings can be evoked only by smell.
- Everything happens in the past tense.
- The main character is a woman named Margaret.
- The ending always makes the reader stop and think.

The Unlettered Simplified Book-Making Process
1. Each team starts a book (bearing in mind the Formula Fundamentals) on page one (not the cover), and thereafter passes the book to the person to the right, but only after being directed to do so by the production trafficker.
2. Before passing, books should be refolded, fan-like, to display only the most recent text and the next (blank) page.
3. Because of an ongoing copyright infringement suit, the letter "e" must not appear anywhere on page one, though it may appear later in the work.
4. In the interest of keeping up with the very latest in literary trends, the production trafficker will periodically announce mandatory literary devices.
5. The eighth person to receive the book is its editor, who will review the entire book and choose a title for the cover.
6. Each editor should then read the team's book aloud to the other teams, and each team must nominate one book for the much-coveted "Pullet Surprise."
7. The team members responsible for the nominated book sign their names on the book. All books, nominated or not, are turned over to the production trafficker.
8. There are no royalties.

    RUNNING THE GAME: Divide your group into teams of eight players. Make sure they understand the rules and how to properly fold the paper after each writer's turn. The time limit is flexible, but teams should have at least 30 minutes to construct their entries. Use your judgment to gauge when the game is winding down, when most teams are nearly finished, etc. When the game is over, collect the books from the editors. Important: Make sure each team has put its team name and its members' names on the back of its entry.

WINNERS: A judge or judges should determine runners-up and winners among the nominated entries, whose names should be read aloud to the group. You might want representatives from the winning teams to come forward and read their own stories, if time permits. You might also wish to let the group determine by applause which are the top five or top three stories. If you have time, you can post the nominated stories (or all of them) in a convenient location where the group can read them before the awards presentation.

Going to Extremes
by Evie Eysenburg (Evita)

Category: trivia/teams/individuals
Players: 24–100+ and one emcee
Playing time: 30–60 minutes
Materials: pens/pencils, paper

A little research is needed, but the effort is well worth it, since almost any number can play and each question has several "right" answers.

PREPARATION: Well before the event, write several simple specific categories for which there are a limited number of answers. For example, one category might be "Colors in a box of 64 Crayola crayons." The players will be asked to come up with two answers: One that is closest to the beginning of the alphabet and one that is closest to the end of the alphabet.

One of the key elements that make this game so user-friendly is that players don't have to have to find the exact best answer, but the closer they are the better. This will be explained in the scoring section below.

Here are some sample categories to start with. You might want to come up with a few that your particular group would find amusing or challenging, such as special categories about a school or a state. Make sure to check your answers in current, accepted reference works, like almanacs or encyclopedias.

Plays of Shakespeare
U.S./Canadian cities with a major league sports team
Disney animated films
U.S. Vice-Presidents
Beatles' top 10 hits
United Nations member countries

Oscar-winning movies
Crimes
European capitals
Campbell soups
Chemical elements
Rock and Roll Hall of Fame members
Spices

BEFORE THE GAME: Allow the players to form teams of two, three, or four, or they can play as individuals. Supply the teams with paper and pencils. Make sure they can't look at each other's answers.

INSTRUCTIONS: Read aloud a series of categories one after the other, allowing time for each category to be answered before reading the next one. Each team (or individual) must write down two items that fit each category. One item should begin with the letter closest to the beginning of the alphabet, the other closest to the end. For example, if the category is Months of the Year, the two answers would be "April" and "September."

SCORING: Points are scored according to each answer's distance from either end of the alphabet, so the object is to score as *few* points as possible. The answer closest to the beginning or end earns 0 points, the second closest 1 point, and so on up the fifth closest, which gets 4 points. Any other answer, or no answer, receives 5 points.

When all categories have been answered, the team with the lowest score wins. Players are responsible for keeping track of their own scores.

RUNNING THE GAME: Be sure the teams clearly understand the rules. During the game, make sure they understand the categories as you read them.

For each category, read the answers aloud when they've been collected. Reading them in reverse scoring order makes the game more exciting. Here's an example, using our 64 crayons category:

"Starting with the beginning of the alphabet, whoever answered 'blue' scores 4 points. Anyone who answered 'black' gets 3 points. The answer 'bittersweet' is worth 2 points. 'Aquamarine' scores 1 point. And 'Apricot,' the closest to the beginning, earns 0 points.

"Now the end of the alphabet. Whoever answered 'white' scores 4 points. 'Wild strawberry' gets you 3 points. If you answered 'yellow' you get 2 points, but 'yellow-green' is worth 1 point. The best answer is 'yellow-orange,' which is worth 0 points."

You should remind players at first that any answers that are not in the top or bottom five earns them 5 points.

WINNERS: Use the process of elimination. Ask every team who scored more than a certain number of points to raise their hands. Then ask for teams who got slightly fewer points, and so on until only one team has their hands raised—the winners!

Chain Reaction

by Henry Hook

Category: trivia/teams
Players: 12–100+ and one emcee
Playing time: 30–60 minutes
Materials: newsprint or other large pieces of paper or cardboard, markers

Based on the bonus round of the bygone TV game show of the same name, Chain Reaction is great for people who can think fast; those who can't can have more time. This game is a double threat: exciting to play and fun to watch!

PREPARATION: The preparation is important but really easy. Make up a list of answers and write each of them on a piece of paper, newsprint, or light cardboard, large enough to be seen from the back of the room. They should be interesting people, places, and things that will be recognized by your group. Collect about twice as many answers as players, which will be enough for one or possibly two games. Here are some examples:

Oprah	lost and found	leap year
computer	Bill Clinton	diamond ring
redhead	Ziploc bag	Las Vegas
James Earl Jones	avocado	*Romeo and Juliet*
stapler	*Goosebumps*	Halloween
kitchen	Monopoly	lipstick
Wal-Mart	Indiana Jones	spaghetti straps
baseball bat	iced tea	Groundhog Day
M*A*S*H	the macarena	tornado

Arrange the players into teams of three, which will play one at a time at the front of the room. You can choose teams randomly or let people pick their own teams. Try to find a playing space with a sound system so that the whole group can hear everything.

INSTRUCTIONS: Each team picks one person to be the guesser; the other two are the clue-

givers. The guesser sits facing the clue-givers and the rest of the group. The emcee sits behind the guesser so that when he holds up a paper, the clue-givers and the audience can see it.

The emcee shows the clue-givers a word or phrase, which they have to describe to the guesser. The catch is that the clue-givers must alternately say one word at a time while making a valid sentence with those words. For example, if the word to be guessed is "Apple," the first clue-giver might say "This," the other clue-giver might say "fruit," then the first says "is," and the other says "red."

If a word in the answer is used in the clues, that answer is invalid and the team tries the next one. The same thing happens if a clue-giver says more than one word at a time. Players may pass on any word.

Each team has one minute to get as many answers as they can. When everyone has had a chance to play, the top five teams have a playoff.

You can make the game just a little more difficult by requiring the sentences that the clue-givers are constructing for the guesser to be questions.

RUNNING THE GAME: You should have one assistant to keep time and another to keep score. If possible, get a microphone for each clue-giver as well as the guesser, so the audience can follow the game and nonplayers will be entertained and not bored.

Audience members are the judges, so if a clue-giver says more than one word or uses a word in the answer, they should speak up. The emcee must decide whether the guesser has correctly guessed the answer. A little leniency might be in order, so that "Help Wanted," for instance, could be acceptable when "Want Ads" was the actual phrase.

KEEP IN MIND: Make sure the timekeeper pays proper attention. Be careful to only reveal one answer at a time.

Two-Player Chain Reaction

by Dwight Freund (Dandr)

Believe it or not, Chain Reaction can be played successfully with two-player teams, where one player knows the answer and the other doesn't. Granted, it's more difficult to get the answers right, but it works!

PREPARATION: The same as for regular Chain Reaction. In fact, you might want to switch over to this version after playing the standard way for a while.

RUNNING THE GAME: Players pair off and take turns playing in front of the assembled group. The emcee holds up the answers behind the guesser while the clue-giver and the guesser try to form a valid sentence, alternately saying one word at a time. As in the regular game, the team tries to get as many answers as possible in 30 or 60 seconds. Scoring is the same as well, though the scores for the regular game shouldn't be measured against those of the two-player game.

The team should decide ahead of time who will start the sentence. It usually works best with the guesser starting, since beginning with "This" is usually helpful.

Sabotage Chain Reaction

by *Thomas Weisswange*

This is the regular three-player-to-a-team version but with a devious twist: player one knows the answer, player two tries to guess the answer, and player three tries to sabotage the efforts of the other two by inserting words to confuse or mislead the guesser. Remember: The resulting sentence must be valid! Be prepared for long, convoluted sentences, though, that may seem somewhat poetic.

In the following example the answer is "Casablanca." Don't forget that even though Marcia does not know the answer, she must try to help Harvey steer the sentence to something useful, while keeping it grammatically correct after Scott's sneaky bombshells.

Marcia (guesser): This.
Harvey (clue-giver): Place.
Scott (saboteur): Flows.
Marcia (guesser): From.
Harvey (clue-giver): Bogart's.
Scott (saboteur): Brain.
Marcia (guesser): When.
Harvey (clue-giver): He.
Scott (saboteur): Can't.
Marcia (guesser): Think.
Harvey (clue-giver): Romantically.
Scott (saboteur): Under.
Marcia (guesser): The.
Harvey (clue-giver): Germans.
Marcia (guesser): Is it "Casablanca"?

RUNNING THE GAME: This game has been played only noncompetitively, but I've come up with a system for scoring, in case cutthroat players insist on playing for bragging rights.

Two teams of two players square off against each other in a duel. While one team is playing, a member of the other team enters as the Saboteur. The team that gets the most answers in one minute wins that particular duel. Winning teams face each other in semi-final and final rounds.

It Takes Two

by Mike Shenk (Manx)

Category: trivia/teams (or individual)
Players: 12–100+, one emcee, one scorekeeper
Playing time: 1–1½ hours
Materials: easel/blackboard, as many yellow, red,
and blue index cards as the number of players

This game is like a live game show, complete with "celebrities." Though there are two large teams, each person contributes in a very individual way.

PREPARATION: Write between 10 and 20 trivia questions. These questions should meet two requirements:

1. The answer to each question must be a specific whole number.

2. The question should require an answer that is hard to know or figure out exactly.

For example, "How many Billboard Top Forty hits did Elvis Presley have?" is an acceptable question, since no one but hard-core Elvis fanatics will know the answer (115). Less good is "How many movies have won the Best Picture Oscar?" because millions of people watch the Oscar TV shows and may know what number show the latest one was.

BEFORE THE GAME: Give everyone three index cards, one each of red, yellow, and blue. Divide the group into two roughly equal teams and ask each to choose a captain. Recruit six "celebrities" to be your panel. These folks won't be competing, but they'll be having fun! You can choose them yourself, ask for volunteers, or even arrange beforehand for six local celebrities (TV weatherperson, mayor, actors, etc.) or eminent people in your playing group (PTA president, school mascot, reverend, etc.).

The celebrities form three two-member teams: a red team, a yellow team, and a blue team.

You'll need a scorekeeper to keep track of the teams' points and the panel's answers on the blackboard.

INSTRUCTIONS: Players pretend they're part of a TV game show called *It Takes Two*. First introduce the celebrity pairs, then explain how the game works.

You (or the emcee if it's not you) will ask the celebrities a few trivia questions that will each be answered by a number. Each celebrity will answer on his or her own, and the two answers will then be averaged to get the answer for that pair. For example, suppose the question is "How many miles long is Lake Michigan?" If Celebrity A answers "420" and Celebrity B says "336," the team answer would be 378, the average of those two numbers. (The real answer is 307 miles.)

When all six celebrities have answered the same question and the averages calculated, the rest of the group (the "audience") votes for the one they think is closest to being correct by holding up the colored card that corresponds to the celebrity pair they're voting for. The two team captains quickly count or estimate the cards and deliver a single vote for their team.

The team who votes for the celebrity pair that came closest to the actual answer earns a point. The team with the most points after a certain number of questions (decide this ahead of time) wins the game.

RUNNING THE GAME: You can round numbers off when averaging answers. A calculator will help crunch the numbers quicker, but it's not really necessary. If a team vote is hard to determine, the emcee and scorekeeper can help the team captain count the cards.

Here are some sample facts that you can use to make good questions. Be sure to check your answers in current, accepted reference works, like almanacs or encyclopedias.

- Top speed of a Zamboni ice resurfacing machine, in m.p.h.? (9)
- Number of words in the Presidential oath of office? (35)
- Length of the Statue of Liberty's nose, in inches? (54)
- Number of spots on Disney's 101 Dalmatians? (3110)
- Length, in hours, of the film *Gone With the Wind*, without editing? (83)

- Number of houses supplied in a Monopoly set? (32)
- Number of English kings and queens since Henry VIII? (21)
- Number of species at the Bronx Zoo? (674)
- Goals scored by Pelé in his career? (1281)
- Number of islands that make up the state of Hawaii? (132)

50-50 Trivia

by Martin Eiger (Wrybosh)

Category: trivia/individuals
Players: 24–100+ and one emcee
Playing time: 1½–2½ hours
Materials: 3" × 5" index cards, answer sheets, pens/pencils, paper

This is a delightfully tricky game for both trivia novices and trivia buffs, neither of whom has an advantage. The object is to come up with a trivia question that will stump exactly half of the other players but will be answered correctly by the other half.

PREPARATION: Prepare enough answer sheets for everyone. They should consist of numbered blanks. If you're not sure how many people will play, overestimate the number of blank spaces.

BEFORE THE GAME: Hand out the answer sheets, pens, pencils, and index cards, one card per player.

INSTRUCTIONS: Every player thinks of a trivia question and writes it on an index card along with the correct answer and the player's name. The question can be on any subject. The object is to think of a question that half the other players will get right and other half will get wrong. The player whose question comes closest to the 50% mark wins the game.

Questions that require short, definitive answers will help move the game along smoothly.

When the players have finished writing their questions (and answers!), collect the cards and start reading the questions. After each question is read, players write their answer in the corresponding blank on the answer sheet. Players should answer their own questions correctly. Remind players to include their names on the answer sheet.

As you read the questions,

number them. Don't reveal who wrote each question just yet. Allow about the same amount of time for answering each question. Keep the cards in order.

When all the questions have been read and the answers recorded, everyone switches answer sheets. Now you're ready to check the percentages.

Every player should now be holding somebody else's answer sheet. Read each question again, name the player who wrote it, and announce the right answer. All players whose answer sheets have that correct answer should raise their hand. Then count the raised hands to see how close to 50% the question scored.

SCORING: Ask someone to keep score or do it yourself. Write down the players' names when you read their questions and then determine the percentage of correct answers. Do this by multiplying the number of correct answers by 100, then dividing the result by the total number of players. Subtract that percentage from 50 to get that player's score. Unless you're playing with exactly 100 people, you might find a calculator useful!

For example, in a game with 85 people, Nicholas writes, "What is the capital of South Dakota?" If 37 people have the correct answer (Pierre), the percentage of correct answers is 37 times 100 divided by 85 equals 43.5%. (You can round your percentages off to the nearest whole number, if you like.) So Nicholas's score is 50 minus 43.5, which equals 6.5.

Find the winner through the process of elimination, as described earlier, or by a quick scan of your scoresheet.

Trivia Quizzes

Trivia quizzes come in many flavors. Here are a few of them.

Elimination

by John Chaneski

Category: trivia/individuals
Players: 12–100+ and one emcee
Playing time: 15–45 minutes
Materials: trivia questions, paper, pens/pencils

This is a dog-eat-dog game where perfection is the rule. It could finish quickly, so be prepared to run several games and then a playoff round.

PREPARATION: In all these trivia games, it will be necessary to prepare questions in advance. Whether you take questions from the Trivial Pursuit game or a trivia book or make them up yourself, get the questions and answers from a current, widely accepted source. Tell your group where you got your trivia.

The game will be more interesting if you gear the trivia to the particular interests of your group. For example, a crowd at a high-school reunion would find questions about the school and the years they attended that school particularly entertaining.

BEFORE THE GAME: Make sure everyone has a sheet of paper, something to write with, and something to lean on, since they'll be standing, not sitting. Have everyone pair off with someone else.

INSTRUCTIONS: This is a no-holds-barred test of trivia knowledge. The game begins with everyone standing up. You will ask a question and every player writes an answer, making sure the partner doesn't see the answer. Players then trade papers with their partner and see what the partner wrote. Then give the correct answer. If a player's partner has written the wrong answer, the partner must sit down.

A seated player is still in charge of checking the partner's answers until he or she sits down. In that case, the two players are out of the competition. The last person standing will be the winner.

DURING THE GAME: Make sure people are playing the game correctly. Depending on what kind of trivia you're using, you might expect some people to have alternate answers that they think are correct. Be prepared to stand by your decisions as to the facts.

SCORING: Play several games, then have the winners stand against each other in a head-to-head playoff to determine King Trivia.

Trivia Baseball
Author unknown

Category: trivia/teams
Players: 12–100+ and one umpire
Playing time: 1–2 hours
Materials: trivia questions, 3" × 5" cards, blackboard, colored tape, colored chalk

Don't assume that Trivia Baseball would appeal only to sports fans. It's just an entertaining and exciting way of running a standard trivia quiz.

PREPARATION: Prepare some trivia. Thematically, baseball or general sports trivia would be fun, but absolutely any kind is appropriate. You'll need four different levels of trivia: easy (singles), medium (doubles), difficult (triples), and really hard (home runs).

Number each question and write them separately on 3" × 5" cards. It might make things easier (for you) to put questions of different levels on cards of different colors. Keep a numbered list of the answers. You'll need 32 questions per inning.

Use the colored tape to make a baseball diamond on the blackboard. It should look something like what's on page 89.

Notice that there are boxes to keep track of outs, as well as boxes for each team's inning score. The more innings in your game, the more the players will be directly involved.

BEFORE THE GAME: Divide the group into two teams of roughly the same size and assign a different color to each. To illustrate the following instructions, we'll assume you have a Red team and a Blue team. (If you have the time and the inclination, prepare paper pennants and such for the teams to wave.)

Each team chooses a captain or "coach," who will remain standing and decide the "batting order." Give both coaches four trivia questions from each difficulty level. Decide which team will be first "at bat."

INSTRUCTIONS: The Red team is up first. Each coach has 16 cards with trivia questions on them. Four are easy, which count as singles; four are medium, which count as doubles; four are hard, which count as triples; and four are very hard, which count as home runs.

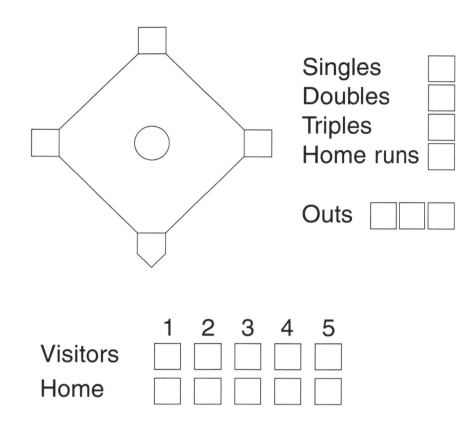

The Red coach will determine the batting order. The coach tells the leadoff batter to stand. This player can choose any difficulty level. The Blue coach and assistant managers (anyone else on the Blue team) decide which question on that level will be "pitched" to the batter.

The batter has 10 seconds (or set a time limit of your choice) to answer the question. If the question is answered correctly, the Red team advances a runner the appropriate number of bases depending on the question's difficulty level. All runners already on base also advance that many bases. If the question is answered incorrectly, Red has one out for that half-inning. After three outs, it's Blue's turn at bat.

There's one more rule you need to keep in mind: though the lead-off batter can choose any difficulty level, the next batter in the lineup must choose from one of the remaining levels. Once all four levels have been chosen, the next batter can again choose any level.

As umpire, you'll be in charge of the answers and keeping track of the runners, the levels, the outs, and the scores on the board. The team with the most runs at the end of the game wins.

DURING THE GAME: At the beginning of each inning, make sure that the "pitching" team's supply of questions is restocked to four of each difficulty level. Besides keeping track of the board, you might very well be in charge of timing the batters, judging the correctness of their answers, and any other umpiring duties. If a team goes through all 16 trivia questions, that team's turn is over.

SCORING: Draw a little stick figure of the appropriate color at home plate every time a team is at bat. If a runner makes it to a base, draw a man of that color on the base. Draw and erase the runners as they make their way around the bases.

Beat the Champ
by Will Shortz

Category: trivia/teams
Players: 24–100+ and one emcee
Playing time: 1–2 hours
Materials: trivia questions, blackboard

PREPARATION: As in the other games, you'll need a lot of trivia on hand, but that's all.

BEFORE THE GAME: Divide the group into two approximately even teams. It'll be easier to run if you put someone else in charge of scoring.

INSTRUCTIONS: One person from each team stands up. You ask them a trivia question. The first to correctly answer the question remains standing and that player's team gets a point. The other player sits down, and two other players from that team stand up. There are now three players standing. You ask another question and, as before, the first person to answer correctly remains standing, while the others sit. But this time the winner earns a point for each opposing player who must sit. Each time a person who is standing alone (a "champ") gets a question right, the opposing team adds an additional person to the next group that stands up. When a person who gets a question right wasn't a champ, the game reverts to one on one. A player who unseats a champ earns his team one point. It might help to think of it this way: every time all the standing members of a team must sit down, the opposing team receives one point for each player that sits.

Continue until a time limit has been reached or a predetermined number of questions have been asked. The team with the highest score at that point wins.

DURING THE GAME: You and the scorekeeper act as judges to determine which person answered first. In the case of a tie, ask another question. All standees remain standing in such a case.

Along with the scores, keep track of the individual players who successfully defend against the most opponents. You can award a prize to the most successful defenders on both the winning and losing teams.

Trivia Hunt
by John Chaneski

Category: trivia/teams/individual
Players: 12–50+ and one emcee
Playing time: 30–60 minutes
Materials: trivia questions, pens/pencils, paper, numbered slips of paper

This game requires players to be very active, so make sure you play it with the type of group that would enjoy it the most. If you think your players are trustworthy, ignore the numbered slips of paper and all references to them.

Unlike other games in this book, Trivia Hunt requires a specialized playing area. It is meant to be played in a library or bookstore since that is where teams will be searching for answers. Trivia Hunt is an appropriate fund-raiser for a public library or promotion for a bookstore. *Do not run this game without the permission of the site that you're planning to use.*

PREPARATION: You'll need at least as many trivia questions as there are players or teams, maybe twice as many, which you'll need to write down in a list, copy, and hand to each of the players just before the game. The trivia should be very tough, to force players to search for the answers. Make sure all the answers can be found where you run the game!

If possible, vary the order of the questions on each list and use a lot of questions. This will help prevent teams from looking for the same answers at the same time.

Be creative with your questions. Here are some examples of different sources for answers that can be found in a library:

Dictionaries	Magazines
Atlases	The card catalogue
Works of fiction	Bibles
Children's books	Phone books
Picture books	Books of quotations

If you're not sure you can trust your players, you'll need numbered slips of paper for every team. Assign each team a number and give its players as many slips of paper, with their team number on them, as there are questions. For example, if you're using 50 questions, Team 1 gets 50 slips of paper numbered "1."

BEFORE THE GAME: Trivia Hunt can be played as individuals or in teams of two or more, depending on the number of players and the general atmosphere you're striving for. Individuals will be quieter than pairs or teams, but it's not as much fun to play alone. Assign each team a number unless you trust your players.

Hand out the lists of questions. In the interest of fairness, have players keep the sheets facedown until they're ready to begin. Hand out the slips of paper, too, if you're using them.

Decide on a time limit to complete the entire list of questions

INSTRUCTIONS: Each team has a list of trivia questions. The answers to every one of them can be found somewhere in this library (or bookstore). Starting on your signal, players will have to search for the answers, write them on their answer sheets, and hand them in.

If you're going to use the numbered slips, here's an additional rule. Even if a player knows an answer off the top of his head, the team still must locate a book where that answer can be found, write the name of the book next to their answer, and place one of their numbered slips in the book, between the cover and first page. Players must then replace the book precisely where they found it.

The team that answers the most questions in the allotted time or hands in the first completely correct set of answers wins the game.

DURING THE GAME: Keep track of the time and the players. If you're not counting on the teams to keep track of their own deadline, you might have to announce the end of the game over a public address system or just spread the word. If you're using a p.a. system, you should also periodically announce how much time remains. Remind your players to be considerate of other players, patrons, and property.

SCORING: Teams get one point for each correct answer. If more than one team has correctly answered all of the questions, the team that handed their answers in first wins.

The purpose of the slips of paper is to keep teams from hiding books from one another. After the answers have been handed in, you or an assistant can check the winning team's sources.

Strange but True

by Fraser Simpson

Category: bluffing/individual (or team)
Players: 25–100+ and one emcee
Playing time: 1–2 hours
Materials: pens or pencils, paper, index cards, oaktag (optional), markers (optional)

This wacky game requires a bit of research but is well worth the effort. Though it's fine for complete strangers, it works best if most members of the group know one another at least a little. The game will provoke some discussion immediately after and perhaps for years to come!

PREPARATION: Tell your group ahead of time that you're preparing for a game and need volunteers who have secrets to reveal. You're not looking for dark or embarrassing secrets, but just interesting and unusual facts about themselves that nobody knows. The best facts are those that no one would ever guess about that person. Here are some examples:

A shy but friendly woman: "In grade school I was a bully."

A working actor: "I once won a prize for selling aluminum siding."

A tall woman: "I was thrown from a horse during equestrian competition."

A young man: "I was the jury foreman on a federal racketeering trial."

Interview volunteers separately and privately. If you decide to use someone's secret in the game, tell that person not to reveal it to anyone else in the group or to say that he or she is part of a game. Once you have collected six or more really good secrets, describe each of them with three short, first-person sentences on an index card, revealing a little more about the secret with each sentence. For example:

Secret A: 1. "I was on a jury of a three-month federal court case."

Secret A: 2. "The trial was to determine if racketeering was involved in the door-to-door candy sales business."

Secret A: 3. "To top it all off, I was the jury foreman."

You might also want to prepare three 1' × 1' oaktag cards bearing the numbers 1, 2, and 3 for each secret.

BEFORE THE GAME: Take the secret-holders aside, one by one, and give each of them a randomly chosen card relating to their own secret.

Also choose two other players from the group for each secret and give them the other two sentences. Instruct everyone you give a sentence to that they must memorize it and be prepared to deliver it in a believable manner when called to the front of the room.

You can add some variety by using some secrets that are gender- or age-specific and some that are not. For example, you'd need three women to relate the story of "giving birth in a taxi during rush hour," but you could use any combination of men and women to tell the tale of "spilling coffee on the President." Sometimes you can write the clues to intentionally obscure the sex and/or age of the secret-holder.

Be sure to keep a reference list for yourself that indicates which extras go along with which secret-holder. For example: Secret A—Nancy (secret-holder), Barbara (extra), and Ellen (extra); Secret B—Stan (secret-holder), Julia (extra), Charlotte (extra); etc.

INSTRUCTIONS: The game is a cross between the old TV game shows *I've Got a Secret* and *To Tell the Truth*. Call three people to the front of the room and give each of them one of the numbered oaktag cards for identification. These three people will reveal information about a secret fact that applies to one of them. When they're done, everyone else in the group guesses whom the secret applies to and writes that person's number on a piece of paper.

The secret-holders are then revealed. Each person in the group earns one point for each correct guess. When it's all over, the best detective will be announced!

RUNNING THE GAME: Call all the "Secret A" crew to the front of the room. Give each of them the oak-tag number card that corresponds to the sentence they'll be delivering and have them stand in order, holding the cards in front of them. You may want to give a little background or humorous introduction to the secret before they recite their sentences. For example, "One of these three people is the last person you'd want to house-sit for you. Let's hear why."

Now ask the reciters to deliver their sentences, allowing time for the other players to absorb what they're hearing. When the third one is done, instruct the players to write down their guesses. When everyone has an answer, the secret-holder identifies him- or herself in whatever grand manner seems the most fun. The other two can turn their backs or sit down and leave the secret-holder standing. Have fun with it.

WINNERS: When all the secrets have been revealed, determine who had the highest score or scores by eliminating the low scores step by step. Ask everyone who got more than three right to raise their hands, then more than four right, then five. Continue until there is only one person left with a raised hand. That's the winner!

Blobs!

by Hubert Phillips

Category: noncompetitive
Players: 12–100+ and one emcee
Playing time: 15–30 minutes
Materials: none

Though nearly impossible to play as a competitive game, Blobs! is great fun for everyone. The object is to detect errors in a story or speech while someone is reading it aloud. Each time a listener hears an error, he or she shouts "Blob!"

PREPARATION: You'll need some writing skills for this or you'll need to recruit someone who has them. The presentation should be interesting and entertaining. This can be accomplished by writing something appropriate for the occasion. Here are a few examples:

- At a family reunion, tell a story of a famous ancestor or a notable event that involved you or another family member.

- At a convention, give some background about the location or tell about some new events or innovations in the conventioneers' field.
- At a party, tell something unique or interesting about the party's honoree, or the history of the occasion.
- In a classroom, give a report on some current event or recently learned subject.

When composing your speech, remember to include many facts as well as errors! There can be many different kinds of errors, including grammatical mistakes, contradictions, blatant omissions, additions, etc. Note in your text where the errors are so that you don't inadvertently miss one yourself. Write the correct version in the margins, in brackets, or on a separate sheet so that you can explain the errors to your players.

Here's a short example of an error-filled Blobs! speech:

"New York is one of my favorite places for theater. I visited three times last year and saw a different show every time. The first show I saw was *Les Misérables*. Though it's the longest-running show in Broadway history [BLOB! *Cats* is the longest-running show], it's not the longest running show in the world. That honor goes to Agatha Christie's *The Mousetrap*. *Les Miz*, based on a book by Walter Hugo [BLOB! Victor Hugo], tells the story of Jean Valjean, a noble man who is imprisoned for stealing a loaf of bread. He is relentlessly pursued by Javert [BLOB! Pronounced zha-VAIR] ..."

You get the idea. Vary the intervals between blobs to keep your audience on their toes. Too many blobs is boring as is not enough blobs. Throw in some errors that are amusing or surprising. Also throw in some amusing and surprising facts.

DURING THE GAME: Since you might be distracted by your attempt to deliver a scintillating presentation, it's a good idea to have an assistant reading over your shoulder who can keep track of blobs in your speech and listen for blobs from the audience.

Remember to clearly state after each blob exactly why a blob is a blob. ("It was Victor Hugo, not Walter Hugo.") If someone shouts out "Blob!" at an inappropriate time, it could be because of a fact you've inserted that may not be generally known. ("True, *The Mousetrap* is really the longest running show.") A wrong blob might also be for an error you didn't know you had! Ask the reason for the shouted blob; maybe the shouter is correct.

SCORING: This game is somewhat free-form. It resists scoring, though you're welcome to try to devise a scoring system for it. Even though it's noncompetitive, your group will find it very much fun.

Mafia

by Anonymous

Category: bluffing/teams
Players: 11, 13, or 15
Playing time: 45+ minutes
Materials: a deck of playing cards

The origins of Mafia, one of the most unusual games in this book, are a mystery. Though difficult to describe and daunting to behold, it is included here because anyone who plays it soon becomes a rabid fan.

PREPARATION: Remember to bring the playing cards.

BEFORE THE GAME: Pull out one red jack, two black number cards, and enough red number cards so that each player will get one card. Shuffle and deal them out, one to a player, and tell players they may look at their card but not show it to anyone else.

A moderator facilitates the night and day modes of the game and expedites votes on assassinations. The first person assassinated acts as moderator for the game.

INSTRUCTIONS: The playing card each player holds reveals the player's role in the game and whether the player is on the Citizen team or the Mafia team. A team wins by killing off every member of the other team.

A player holding a numbered card in a red suit is a Citizen of the town. The player with the red jack is the Night Commandant, who is also a Citizen and works on the Citizens' behalf.

A player with a numbered card in a black suit is a member of the Mafia. There are only two of these. Although the Mafia are seriously outnumbered, rest assured that they have a big advantage in this game and end up winning more often than not.

The game advances mostly through discussions, which take place over several "days," between which are "night" times when the Mafia and Night Commandant ply their trades. When players' eyes are open and they are talking, that's daytime.

The game begins on the first day, when the discussion produces the identity of a person to be assassinated. Players decide who to assassinate based on actions and words of other players. (If someone is quiet, does that mean he's a Citizen or Mafia? That's for you to decide.) The first assassination can seem arbitrary, but the victim gets to moderate the rest of the game. The discussion of the first assassination gives clues that will help players make later decisions. (If a player quickly votes to assassinate a player, does that mean he's a Citizen or Mafia? Again, that's for you to decide.)

A person can be assassinated only when a majority of the players agree that the assassination of that person will take place (the person who is to be assassinated gets a vote). If a player at any time thinks a majority may be ready to assassinate another player, he or she goes to the moderator, who will call for a vote by a show of hands in favor of the assassination (the first time, when there is no moderator, any player can call for a vote). If there is no majority the discussion continues; if the majority rules in favor, the assassination takes place.

A player killed by vote is allowed "final words." The victim may say anything at all, and if the player is the Night Commandant, those last words can be very important. Once the final words are said, though, the assassinated player may not speak at all for the rest of the game.

Once a person has been killed, night falls, at which point the following actions take place. The moderator will guide the group through these actions. Here is what happens, in order:

1. All players close their eyes and begins softly humming and swaying back and forth (to camouflage any movements that occur at night).
2. On the moderator's signal, the Mafia members (only!) open their eyes and silently identify each other.
3. The Mafia members indicate one player whom they want to assassinate.
4. The moderator acknowledges their choice by nodding "yes."
5. The Mafia members close their eyes.
6. The Night Commandant (the player with the red jack) opens his or her eyes when told to do so by the moderator.
7. The Night Commandant wordlessly indicates another player that he or she wants information about.

8. The moderator indicates whether that person is Mafia: a nod means "yes," a shake of the head means "no."
9. The Night Commandant closes his or her eyes.
10. The moderator tells everyone to open their eyes.
11. The moderator informs the Mafia's victim of his or her untimely demise. Mafia victims do not get final words but simply reveal their card and do not speak again. Then the discussion and the game continue with another day.

As the game progresses, the Night Commandant (if still alive) knows more and more about who is Mafia and who isn't. He (or she) needs to steer the conversation toward the assassination of Mafia members with or without revealing that fact that he is the Night Commandant. But the Mafia will almost certainly assassinate the Night Commandant at their first opportunity, so revealing one's Night Commandant status is a tough decision. Of course, people can lie and say they're the Night Commandant when they aren't. Determining who's being truthful is part of the game.

The game ends when the last member of either team is assassinated. The survivor's team wins (so you can win even if you are dead). It is very possible that a single remaining Mafioso can remain alive through several days and win the game through guile and deception.

Mafia is a game best explained through playing. It is a fascinating, frustrating, and often hilarious game that incorporates group psychology, logic, bluffing, acting, and wits.

KEEP IN MIND: Mafia can take a while, especially with a large group and good players. Sometimes a player will suggest an assassination just to get the game moving. Often this just serves as fodder for further discussion, as the paranoid players question that player's motives, but such suspicion and discussion is usually good for moving the game along.

The Liar's Club

by John Chaneski

Category: bluffing/individuals
Players: 12–100+ and one emcee
Playing time: 1+ hours
Materials: index cards in four colors, white index cards, scoresheets, writing materials

Based on a game show, The Liar's Club is a good opportunity for players to amaze and confound their friends. If you have a few extroverts lying around, you're in for a very good time, though some preparation work is required.

Liar's Club is run like a panel game show, much like It Takes Two (page 82). Players try to determine which panelist is truthfully describing the purpose or source of a mysterious object.

PREPARATION: Look around. If you know four people who are good at making up stories, telling jokes, or thinking on their feet, you might have a decent group of liars. The latter quality isn't too important, since you can prepare several objects (and fake stories to go with them) ahead of time.

You should try to find at least 10 unusual, mysterious objects for your panel to use. Here are five fruitful possibilities:

1. Do it yourself. Go to junkyards, friends' garages, or your own garage. You may be able to rent strange objects, or parts of objects, from interesting antique shops. Be sure to find out what the mystery items really are when you get them and that your source is reliable!

2. Do it yourself ... with help. Ask your selected panel to help you track down objects. Remind them that sources of information must be reliable!

3. Let your players do it. Write a letter or e-mail explaining the game

and distribute it to your group. Ask them to come up with unusual things. This will give you more items to choose from, but the information about such items could be inaccurate or totally wrong. Use this option cautiously!

4. Combine options 1, 2, and 3.

5. Use pictures. If you're strapped for objects, consider researching unusual machines and gadgets at the library. You could create poster-size pictures of the items or hand out a booklet of photocopied images. Number them for easy reference.

If you're lucky, you might find the out-of-print game called Bluffer's Beware. A board-game version of The Liar's Club, it contains dozens of black-and-white drawings of unusual items, along with their uses.

For each mystery object you collect, write down its true purpose on a white index card and fake explanations on three other white cards. To make the game more fun for the panelists, don't let them know whether they're reading the real story or one of the fakes. (But make sure that you, as the host, remember which are the real ones!) For a really exciting game, let them come up with bluffs on their own!

Just because your panel will have written stories in front of them doesn't mean they won't need some skill at bluffing. The whole idea is for the panel to have some fun embellishing the stories and making the whole process entertaining. If you end up using objects brought in by players, your panel will get the chance to come up with off-the-cuff explanations. Good luck!

The scoresheets needed are very simple. They should feature one scoring box for each item you plan to use. It should look something like this:

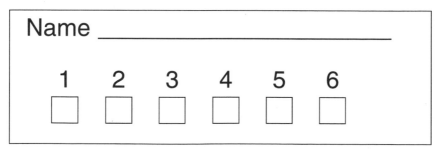

BEFORE THE GAME: You may want to display your mystery items on a table so that the players can get a look at them up close, but this is not mandatory. If you do this, don't let anyone handle the objects.

Give each player a scoresheet and one index card in each of the four colors. This is how they will vote for the panelist they believe is telling the truth. You can have colored signs made up in advance with the panelists' names on them, or arrange for the panelists to wear their particular color.

INSTRUCTIONS: Introduce your panel. Display a mystery item to the group and give it to the panel. Each panelist examines the object and describes or explains it. Only one of them will tell the truth, however, and it's up to the group to decide which one it is. When all four panelists have had their say, briefly summarize their explanations and ask the group to vote.

Call out the numbers 1, 2, 3, and 4, referring to the individual panelists. After each number, players who believe that panelist is the truthful one raise the card of the appropriate color. Quickly estimate which panelist has earned the most votes and keep track of the votes. You might want to practice the counting and voting. Votes cannot be changed!

The best liar—that is, the panelist who lied but got the most votes—earns one point.

When the truth-teller is revealed, the voters for that panelist keep their hands in the air while everyone else lowers theirs. Players with their hands raised will need someone else to mark their scoresheets by putting an X in the correct place. This way everyone can keep track of each other's scores and keep each other honest.

DURING THE GAME: Be an emcee. Banter with the panelists (just as they should banter with each other and the audience). Keep track of the scoring.

WINNERS: Several winners are possible, both on stage and off. The audience winner is the person who guessed the truth-teller the most times. As for the panelists, reward the best liar and any particularly creative or amusing lies.

The Honesty Game
Traditional

Category: team
Players: 16–100 and one emcee
Playing time: 1–2 hours
Materials: none

This game lives up to its name. The honor system is in effect here. A large group of adults who know each other well is the best crowd.

PREPARATION: None.

BEFORE THE GAME: Divide your players into two, three, or four teams of equal size with at least eight people on each team. Call them Team A, Team B, etc. Ask everyone to stand. Appoint a scorekeeper or keep score yourself.

INSTRUCTIONS: Players will know one another a lot better once this game is over. Team A begins. They'll have one minute to talk among themselves and try to come up with an experience that no team member has had but that they believe at least two people on each of the other teams have had. For example, Team A might say, "None of us has been to Alaska." If there are two people on Team B who have been to Alaska, then one person on Team B must sit down and is out of the game. Go through the same process with the other teams. If no other team includes two members who have been to Alaska, then one person on Team A sits down and is out of the game.

Remind players that they're using the honor system and that many players know each other well. Anyone caught in a lie is out of the game!

When there's only one team with any members still standing, the game is over and that team is the (rather inexperienced) winner.

DURING THE GAME: Keep track of the time. Keep score. Keep a watchful eye out for shady claims and decide what constitutes a fair experience. For example, an all-male team that claims "We have never given birth" while playing against a team consisting solely of mothers might be judged unfair.

SCORING: The game scores itself. The last team standing is the winner.

Charades

Following are rules for classic charades and two variations.

Classic Charades

Traditional

Category: team
Players: 12–30+ and one emcee
Playing time: 1–2+ hours
Materials: index cards, pens/pencils, stopwatch

Though charades is not necessarily meant for a huge group, it can be

managed with a few dozen people. Despite the fact that only one person can charade at a time, that player's antics are usually entertaining enough to keep the whole crowd interested and amused. You'll need to know the basic rules of charades to play the variants that follow.

PREPARATION: You can either think of a few charades beforehand or leave the thinking to the players. Write each charade clearly on one index card and include its category. Some common sources for charade challenges:

Films and film quotes
Books and book quotes

TV shows and TV show quotes
Songs and song lyrics
Band names and album titles
Famous quotations
Commercial slogans
Famous people
Magazine titles
Organizations
Poem and essay titles and quotes

Most gamers' groups like to agree on a word limit for each charade. A good limit is 10 (since you have only 10 fingers to indicate the number of words!). Obscure phrases and foreign words are usually considered unfair, but that's for your group to determine.

Some groups like to prohibit the performance of a charade that someone on that team devised, but some groups allow it. If you try to catch the opposing team by tossing an extremely hard charade into the pool, your own team could get stuck with it. The "anything goes" philosophy therefore keeps the difficulty at a manageable level.

BEFORE THE GAME: Divide your players into two, three, or four teams of approximately equal size, give each team a name or number, and make sure everyone has enough index cards and writing utensils, since they'll need to write down the charades they come up with. The number of charades each person puts into the charade pool depends on how many players there are and how long you want the game to last.

Appoint a scorekeeper or keep score yourself. Decide on a maximum time limit for each charade. You should allow at least two minutes and at most five minutes. You may change this later to make it easier or harder on your players.

It's a good idea to have a judge or two, separate from the scorekeeper, whose job it will be to listen for the answer from the guessing team.

INSTRUCTIONS: Tell the players how many charades to come up with; make sure that they write each one separately on an index card along with its source ("*Saturday Night Live* TV Show," for example). Have them fold each card in half and put their team name and author name on the outside. The charade's author may have to act out his or her own charade but is prohibited from guessing it, of course.

Once you've collected enough charades, start the game. Ask a volunteer from the first team to come to the front of the room and pick a charade at random. That person will be the first performer. (If you're not following the "anything goes" method, a charade created by the performer's own team must be put back and another one chosen.) If the author of the charade is someone on the performer's team, that person may not attempt to guess the charade.

The teams take turns. While one team is playing, the other teams are to be quiet. Every player must take a turn at performing.

Explain that when performing they have no more than two minutes (or whatever time limit you determine) to get their team to say the exact words on the index card. The performer may make no sounds whatever and may use no props other than the clothes they're wearing. After silently reading the charade, the performer will have 15 seconds to think about it before the timer starts.

The guessing team may ask the performer questions, but the performer may not respond verbally.

If the charade is correctly guessed, the guessing team scores the number of seconds left on the performer's time. If the charade is not correctly guessed within the time limit, the team gets no points.

DURING THE GAME: Keep the performers and charades moving at a good pace. Make sure that each person on every team gets a chance to perform. Watch the time and make sure the players follow the rules.

When the play has gone on long enough and each team has had an equal number of chances to charade, announce the end of the game. Warn the players when the end is near, so that they can redouble their efforts on their last charade!

SCORING: When the game is over, add up the leftover time that each team has scored. The team with the highest score wins the game.

Tag-Team Charades
Author unknown

Category: team
Players: 30–100+ and one emcee
Playing time: 1–2+ hours
Materials: index cards, pens/pencils, stopwatch

This charades variant will keep a big group hopping. Play is mostly the same as classic charades but with one super (party game) difference. Try this variation if your group is really good at charades.

PREPARATION: Same as classic charades.

BEFORE THE GAME: Same as classic charades, but with no time limit.

INSTRUCTIONS: Once you have the desired number of charades in the pool, explain the basic rules of charades and ask the first performer to come to the front of the room.

After the performer has silently read a chosen charade, start timing 30 seconds. When 10 seconds remain, say "ten seconds" and count down the last five seconds aloud: "Five, four, three, two, one." In those last five seconds, the performer must tag another member of his or her team and whisper the charade to the new performer. That player then takes the stage and continues working on the same charade. The time is reset to 30 seconds, and in the last five remaining seconds that player must tag another player from the same team and hand off the charade.

Naturally, a player who has performed a particular charade may not guess it, and may not be tagged to perform that charade again.

If the charade is guessed before you run out of players, that team scores the number of seconds it took to get the answer. If there are no players left to perform and the charade has not been guessed, that team scores all the seconds they took, plus an extra 60 seconds.

DURING THE GAME: This variation requires you to be very organized. Make sure your timekeeper and judges are very capable and focused. Help the tags and switches go off smoothly and quickly. Make sure newly tagged performers have a few seconds to gather their wits. Make sure that the basic charade rules are followed.

When scoring a team's time, remember that they receive however many seconds the successful performer spent charading, plus 30 seconds for every other player-performer that has acted out that particular charade.

When the play has gone on long enough and each team has had an equal number of chances to charade, announce the end of the game.

SCORING: The team with the lowest score wins.

Mirror Charades
by Rick Rubenstein (Rastelli)

Category: team
Players: 12–30+ and one emcee
Playing time: 1–2+ hours
Materials: index cards, pens/pencils

Like classic charades, Mirror Charades is not necessarily a game for a very large group, but it has a unique twist that makes it a little more challenging.

PREPARATION: Same as for classic charades.

BEFORE THE GAME: Same as classic charades. Decide on a time limit.

INSTRUCTIONS: Same as classic charades, except that there are two performers for every charade. The player who reads the charade (the performer) stands behind his or her team, unseen by them. Another player (the mirror) stands in front of the team; the mirror is the only player on the active team who can see the performer. While the performer acts out the charade, the mirror silently mirrors the performer's motions. The team must get its information from the mirror player only and may not look at the performer for any reason, not even to ask a question.

If the charade is correctly guessed, the guessing team scores the number of seconds left on the time. If it's not correctly guessed within the time limit, the team receives no points. The team with the highest score wins.

DURING THE GAME: Same as classic charades.

SCORING: Same as classic charades. You may want to keep track of each performer/mirror team's times and give an award to the most efficient team.

Game Index

About the Author

John Chaneski, a native of Hoboken, New Jersey, has a long history of playing and creating games, going all the way back to his reign as world Peekaboo champion of 1963–64. A graduate of New York University's Tisch School of the Arts,  he has parlayed a degree in drama into a perplexing career writing puzzles, articles, and reviews for such magazines as *Games, Home Office Computing, React,* Nickelodeon's *GAS,* and Consumer Reports' *Zillions,* among others. He also writes entertainment trivia for CNN.com and other Web sites.

Fan club members will recall his appearances on f/X, CourtTV, HBO, and as Tim Robbins's hand double in the movie *I.Q.* Chaneski also acts, sings, performs stand-up, and writes comedy, fiction, and essays. He is available for $1,000-a-plate benefit dinners, late-night talk shows, and as a host for super party games.